.

電子書提款機

eBook ATM

Johnny Wang

第 2 步: 內容創建 - 寫什麼內容? 46

內容大綱製作(TOC) 46

內容寫作 51

內容確認 (COPYSCAPE) 62

電子書製作 63

第 3 步: 上架行銷 - 去哪賣電子書? 72

如何使用本書

我已經盡可能的把我所知道與我的經驗用我認為最簡單的方式與大家分享，本書有談到英文的部分，我都盡可能的翻成中文，如對本書英文部分還是有疑慮或看不懂的話，建議先上 Google 翻譯去查查看。

目前也可以在亞馬遜上上架繁體中文電子書，中文部分可自行輸入或利用 Google 搜尋相關資料。

不論你是新手、已有販賣電子書或是網路賺錢的經驗，可能的話，請先把這本書至少看過兩遍，再自行操作本書所提到的步驟。

關於我

大家好，我是 Johnny，電子書提款機的作者以及自助出版學院的創辦人，如果你正在看這本書，你可能跟我幾年前一樣，希望能夠找到一些方法，去增加自己的收入，尤其是被動收入。

又或許你是想要將你心中的那本書出版出去，無論是要留做紀念或是去幫助別人，那我要恭喜你，因為福特汽車的創辦人亨利福特曾說: 不管你想你可以或不可以，你都是對的，如果你相信你自己做得到，你一定會達到你自己設定的目標。

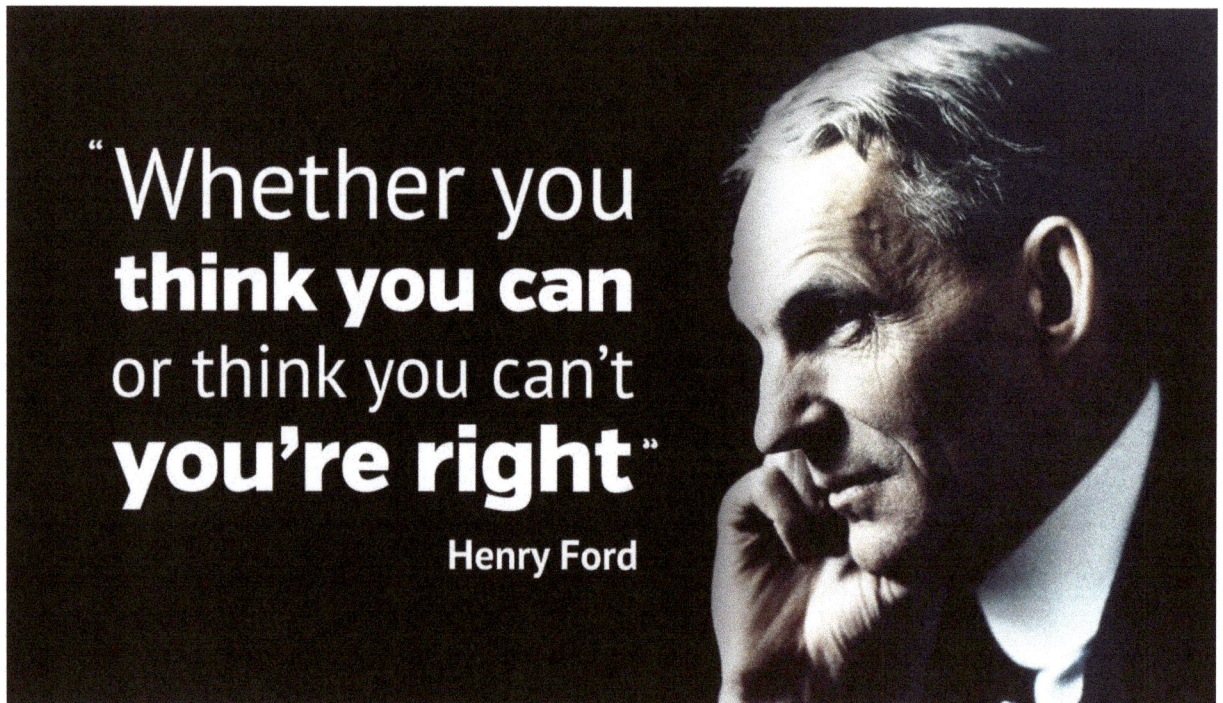

「Whether you think you can or think you can't you're right」
Henry Ford

希望在不久的將來，無論你的目的為何，我都希望能夠看到你的書，到時候記得與我分享。您可以到這裡貼上您書的連結，我們非常歡迎！

有關於我是如何踏進出版這行，我很快的跟大家說明一下，我相信我跟大部分的人一樣，總是希望每個月可以多一些的收入，所以大約在 2012 年就開始在網路上搜尋如何增加收入的資訊。也不知怎麼的因緣際會，可能是吸引力法則的關係，就投入了網路賺錢(網賺)的行列。

我很幸運，大概在從事網賺第二個月的時候，就在 Clickbank 成功地賺到了我有生以來的第一次在網路上賺到的第一筆佣金，美金$17.98。雖然只是少少地$18 美金不到，卻開啟了我的網賺人生之路。

Weekly Sales Snapshot

Week Ending	Gross Sales
2009-12-09 (current week)	$0.00
2009-12-02	$17.98
2009-11-25	$0.00
2009-11-18	$0.00
2009-11-11	$0.00

Daily Sales Snapshot

Mon	Dec	07	$0.00
Sun	Dec	06	$0.00
Sat	Dec	05	$0.00
Fri	Dec	04	$0.00
Thu	Dec	03	$0.00
Wed	Dec	02	$0.00
Tue	Dec	01	$0.00
Mon	Nov	30	$0.00
Sun	Nov	29	$0.00
Sat	Nov	28	$17.98
Fri	Nov	27	$0.00
Thu	Nov	26	$0.00

附註: Clickbank 就像是台灣的通路王(iChannel) 一樣，只是它賣的都是資訊產品，如果不知道什麼是通路王，可以按這裡去看看。

之後就埋頭苦幹地做 Clickbank 的聯盟行銷 (Affiliate Marketing)。跟很多人一樣，雖然賺得到錢，但賺到的錢並不是特別多，所以我又嘗試了各種不同的網賺方法， Clickbank，Google Adsense 廣告點擊，亞馬遜聯盟行銷 (Amazon affiliate)，MarketHealth.com ...等等，這些我都試過。

會這麼堅持地在做網賺，實在是它的自由度太令人著迷 (Obsessed)，因為網賺具有下面的特性：

- 起頭成本低

- 賺到的錢是沒有限制的 (我自己的最高紀錄是一天賺到超過美金$2,500,這是我當上班族想都想不到的,也可能是永遠無法辦到的)
- 沒有地域性的限制 (可以在任何地方從事網賺,只要你有一台電腦跟網路連線)

話說回來,數位產品(Digital Products),廣告,實體產品推廣我都做過,雖然都有賺到錢,但老實說大約都是每月幾百到上千美金不等,每個月的網賺收入並不穩定,再加上 Google 老大的搜尋結果,也就是排名演算法一直再做修正,所以老實說每個月的收入變化有時候也是挺大的。

一直到 2012 年三四月左右,受到 Google 的 Penguin 演算法(Google 的一種搜尋排名演算法的更新)的影響,我從傳統架設網站去推廣產品,賺取佣金的生意模式有了比較大的變化,我才開始比較認真投入亞馬遜 Kindle 電子書出版平台 (Amazon KDP),很幸運地,從 2012 年 12 月開始,我的電子書版稅月收入有了以下爆發性的成長。

Flirting Tips B00ATS18S	70%	2	0	2	N/A	2.99	2.99	0.21	0.03	4.14
21 Steps to B00ATS1A5	70%	1	0	1	N/A	2.99	2.99	0.26	0.04	2.06
Truth about B00ATS1BI	70%	2	0	2	N/A	2.99	2.99	0.34	0.05	4.12
Looking You B00ATS1C6	35%	1	0	1	N/A	2.99	N/A	N/A	N/A	1.05
Total Royalty for sales on Amazon Kindle US Store (USD)										9255.44

Floating My B00B534O4	35%	25	3	22	N/A	0.99	N/A	N/A	N/A	7.70
Floating My B00B534O4	KOLL	N/A	N/A	6	0.0008	N/A	N/A	N/A	N/A	13.39
Floating My B00B534O4ee - Promoti	431	1	430	N/A	0.99	0.00	N/A	N/A	0.00	
Total Royalty for sales on Amazon Kindle US Store (USD)										8322.13

上面兩個截圖是 2012 年 12 月與 2013 年 1 月的兩個月的電子書收入, 2012 年 12 月有$9,255 美金,2013 年 1 月有$8,322 美金,這兩個月平均下來,一個月的收入大約是台幣 26 萬左右。

在這裡不是要跟大家炫耀,而是要讓大家知道,自助出版的版稅收入很可怕,我可以做到,我相信只要你按照本書的方法一步步地去做,你也可以。我的朋友以及與我討論過電子書的網賺同好,他們利用我分享給他們的方法,也從亞馬遜也賺到了數百元到上千元美金不等的電子書版稅佣金收入。

在這邊附上最近的版稅佣金收入：

這樣一個月也有超過$10，000 美金的版稅佣金收入，這幾年來每個月大多有超過$3，000 美金的收入，所以我認為以長期來說，這個網路賺錢生意模式是一種相對穩定賺取被動收入的方式。

但是重點不是在我，**最重要的是，你要能夠持之以恆**，無論你選擇哪一種網路賺錢方式，你必須要不間斷地採取有效行動才行，不是你選擇的方法無效，實在是有太多人無法持續，因為我看過太多人說，他們想要透過網路賺錢，可不可以請我教他，但是最後都沒有恆心，有的是遇到問題(如英文)就放棄，有的是看到別的機會，覺得好像更好，於是就停止行動，無論如何，你千萬不要當那樣子的人，切記切記！！！

在這裡，我即將跟你分享如何從亞馬遜 Kindle 電子書 (Amazon KDP) 去出版你的電子書，並且有機會賺到你想賺到的錢，別懷疑，**我的每月版稅收入只是小 case，國外有許多的人是每個月上百萬台幣的收入**。

如果你也想每個月多賺個幾百美金或上千美金，甚至更多，照著以下步驟做，絕對有機會達到，我自己就在 2012 年 7 月的時候 (大約從事 Amazon KDP 電子書銷售四個月左右)就有上千美金的版稅佣金收入了，想要知道我是怎樣辦到的嗎? 繼續讀下去，你就會知道。

附註: 本內容討論之所有方法僅針對亞馬遜 KDP 平台做探討，蘋果 iBookstore 或其他平台不在本內容討論範圍之內。

為什麼要做電子書

如果你是想從網路上賺錢的或是有一些網賺的經驗，你一定知道，要從網路上賺到錢，必須具備三項要素:

- 產品 (解決方案)
- 網站 (介紹人)
- 流量 (客戶需求)

傳統的網路賺錢或是聯盟行銷的方式是做一個網站，然後想辦法導流量 (人氣) 到網站裡去賣產品或是賺取廣告點擊(如 Google Adsense)，也有所謂的聯盟行銷 (Affiliate Marketing)，就是去代理別人的產品，透過網路(不論是自己建立網站或打廣告)賣給消費者，然後賺取佣金，無論是哪種方法，都需要**產品**，**網站**與**流量**這三項要素，而這三項要素最難取得的就是流量。

但流量取得了，還有一項更重要的項目，那就是**轉換率**，能不能有效的把流量轉成實際的客戶，那又是另外一門學問了。

而電子書不是最近才有的產品，但因為亞馬遜的 Kindle (Kindle 是亞馬遜公司自己推出的平板，就像是蘋果的 iPad 一樣)閱讀器的推出，以及蘋果 iPad 的熱賣，現在在亞馬遜上販賣電子書，有許多比傳統網賺更多的優勢，在網路賺錢的三項要素裡，我認為只要你的產品做的好(也就是電子書，包含好的內容與做好競爭分析)，網站與流量，亞馬遜都會提供給你，所以我個人認為從事電子書銷售比傳統的網賺方便太多了。

而轉換率就看你整個銷售漏斗是如何設計了，我們來看一下傳統網賺與亞馬遜電子書的比較：

	傳統網賺	亞馬遜電子書
產品	需要自己製作或代理其他人產品	只需要製作電子書 (但可外包)
網站	需要做許多網站優化 (SEO) 與維護網站	無須製作網站，上傳亞馬遜平台 (KDP) 即可， 10-15 分鐘即可
流量	需要長時間經營或花錢買流量	亞馬遜免費幫你行銷提供免費流量
優點	網站或關鍵字如果在搜尋引擎排名高，收入可觀 長期來看，如果是長青市場，時間經營夠久，應該會有不錯的固定收入	成本低，電子書越多，收入越高，收入可不斷增加 電子書閱讀器量產化，市場無可限量 ($$) 亞馬遜提供免費流量 亞馬遜幫你行銷電子書
缺點	搜尋引擎演算法改變 - 收入不穩定 整體成本與電子書比起來成本較高 免費流量不易取得	需要製作一定數量高品質的電子書

傳統網賺方式的成本雖然比起實體店面 (如加盟 7-11) 比起來便宜多了，相對於電子書來說，還是一筆不少的花費，通常做好一個網站也許要花到幾千到數萬元台幣不等，而且時間相對來說也比做電子書來的長，我個人認為 (不一定是對的)，由於目前網站太多太過於競爭，想要從網站上賺到可觀的收入難度提高了許多，而對於電子書來說，不但相對來說成本比較便宜(一本書只要約$50-$200 美金或自己寫 = 免費)，而且目前正處於一個上漲的趨勢，如下圖：

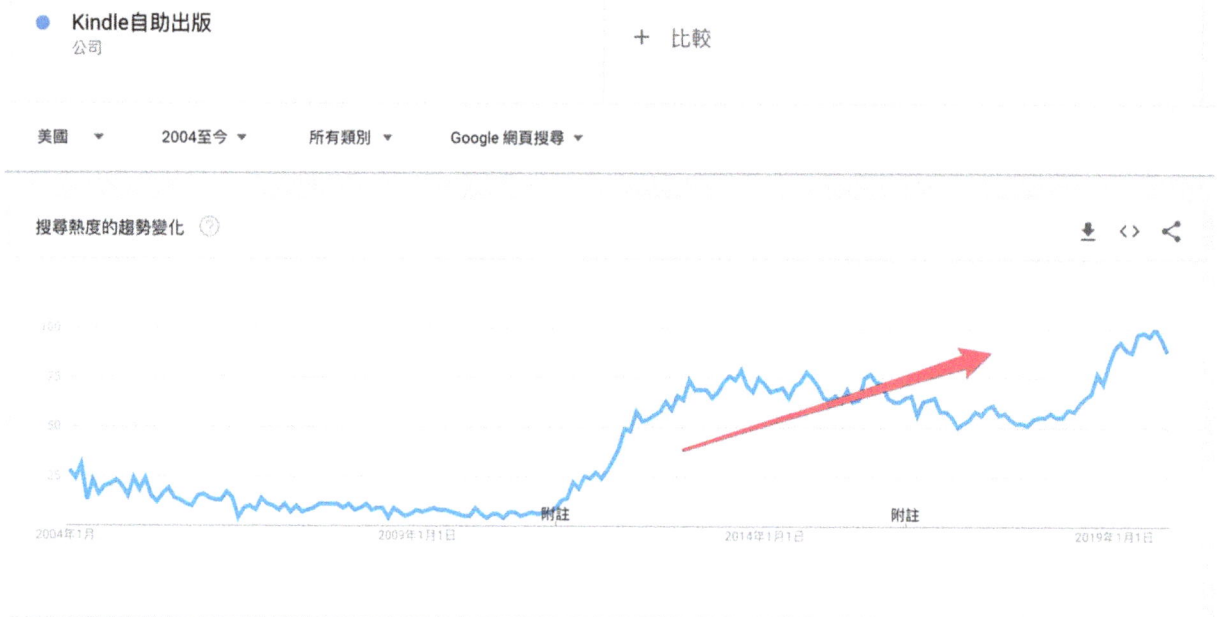

相較於傳統網賺來說，這是一個千載難逢的好機會。再來亞馬遜還會提供你一些流量，還有免費的行銷工具來幫著你行銷，你要做的不過就是把你做好的電子書上架而已，比起傳統網賺來說，我認為比較簡單。

電子書如何賺錢

做電子書，要如何賺錢呢? 原則上就是把我們創作好的電子書，自己當出版商，上架到亞馬遜電子書銷售平台 (Kindle Direct Publishing，簡稱 KDP 平台) 賺取電子書的版稅。一旦我們賣出我們的電子書，亞馬遜就給我們一定比例的版稅佣金，就這麼簡單。

如果你有自己透過傳統出版商出書的經驗，你應該知道，可賺取的版稅最多就是大約實體書本賣價的 15%，但是如果我們是透過亞馬遜電子書銷售平台(Amazon KDP)的話，最多我們可以賺取 70%的版稅!

出版銷售三大步驟

我們要做電子書，首先要先了解整個流程為何？然後再一步步地把流程中的每個步驟做好。

首先我們要做的就是選定主題，也就是利基市場調查，知道要寫甚麼書，甚麼內容，確定好後，再來就是作內容創建，就是去請外包寫作或自己創作，最後一步就是把電子書上架去賣，也就是所謂的上架行銷，就這麼簡單，我把整個亞馬遜電子書銷售的流程簡化為以下的三大步驟：

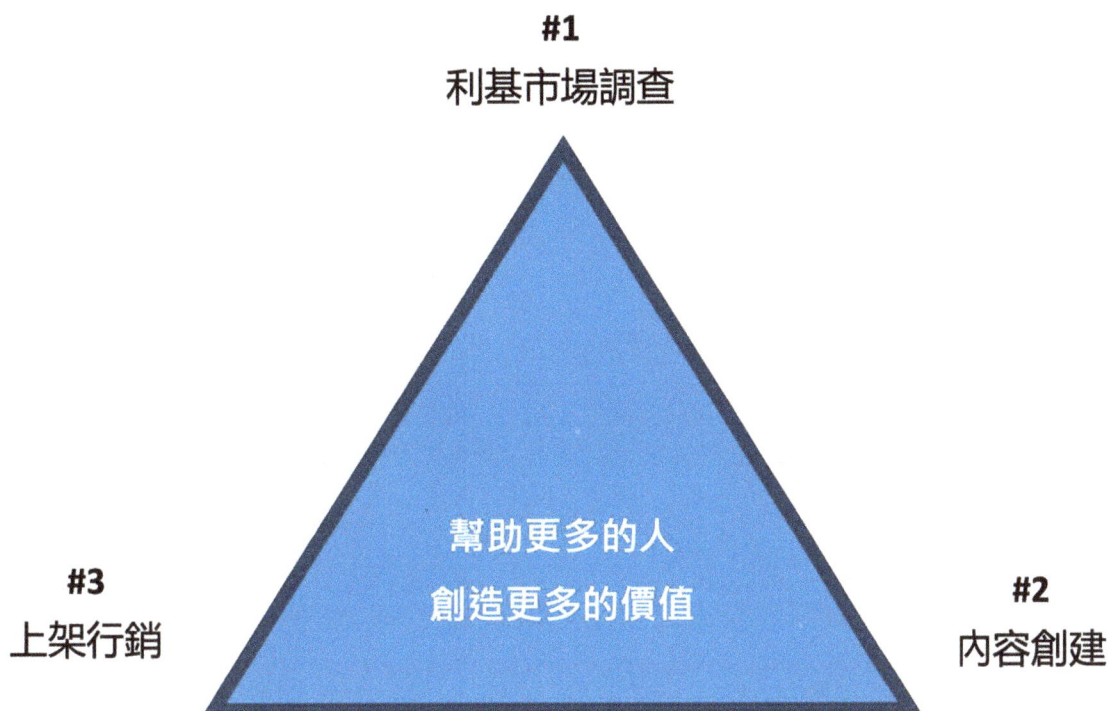

#1
利基市場調查

幫助更多的人
創造更多的價值

#3
上架行銷

#2
內容創建

第 1 步: 利基市場調查 - 寫什麼書?

無論是做電子書或是其他網賺，第一步就是要確定你的利基市場，以出版來說，也就是要寫什麼書? **而且是要知道寫哪些書才會賣的好**，很多時候你可能出版了很多書，但最後卻賣得不好，那就是利基市場的分析沒有做好。

也就是你誤認為大家都覺得你的東西好，這是沒人買你的書的第一個關鍵，所以首先我們要做的第一步就是去做市場的分析。

附註: 一般來說，在亞馬遜 KDP 平台上以小說類的書比較暢銷，但對新手來說非小說類的電子書比較好上手，所以這裡談到的先以非小說類的書為主。

但是要寫甚麼樣的書呢？我們可以用下面幾個方式來先找市場：

問自己需要什麼？自己會什麼？

你可以問自己會甚麼？或是需要甚麼？因為通常你自己的需要，別人也有可能有相同的需求，比如說：

- 我怎麼樣可以自然受孕？
- 我如何上台講話的時候不會緊張？
- 我如何利用 Wii 來幫助我減肥？
- 我如何跟我的家人有更好的關係？
- 我如何在工作上能夠更成功？
- 我要怎樣才能夠從網路上賺到錢？
- 我要怎麼樣才能學會彈鋼琴？
- 我要如何才能增加重量並有強壯的體格？

有一些想法了嗎？這些都是你可以讓自己去多想想的一些例子，多問問自己，或者是家人與朋友，看看他們有沒有其它的問題或者是其它的需求是你可以在網路上找到有相關的產品來符合他們的需求。

讀到這裡後，從現在開始你應該要是去注意你周遭相關的人士，對甚麼有興趣或是有甚麼問題是他們想解決的，這些都有可能是會在亞馬遜裡大賣的電子書。

利用最佳銷售排行榜找電子書主題

在尋找亞馬遜電子書利基市場最快也是最簡單的方式就是到 Amazon 的最佳銷售排行榜 (Amazon Bestsellers)去看看到底有什麼電子書是現在在市場上熱賣的。

你可以看到下圖左側欄位裡的分類：

然後點選你有興趣或是你認為可能是有市場的分類去看看。

比如說我點選進去 Kindle eBooks 裡頭 Nonfiction (非小說)的分類，你可以看到會有更細部的分類出現，可以在你認為有潛力的分類再點選進去看看，例如：Kindle ebooks-> Nonfiction -> Health，Fitness&Dieting

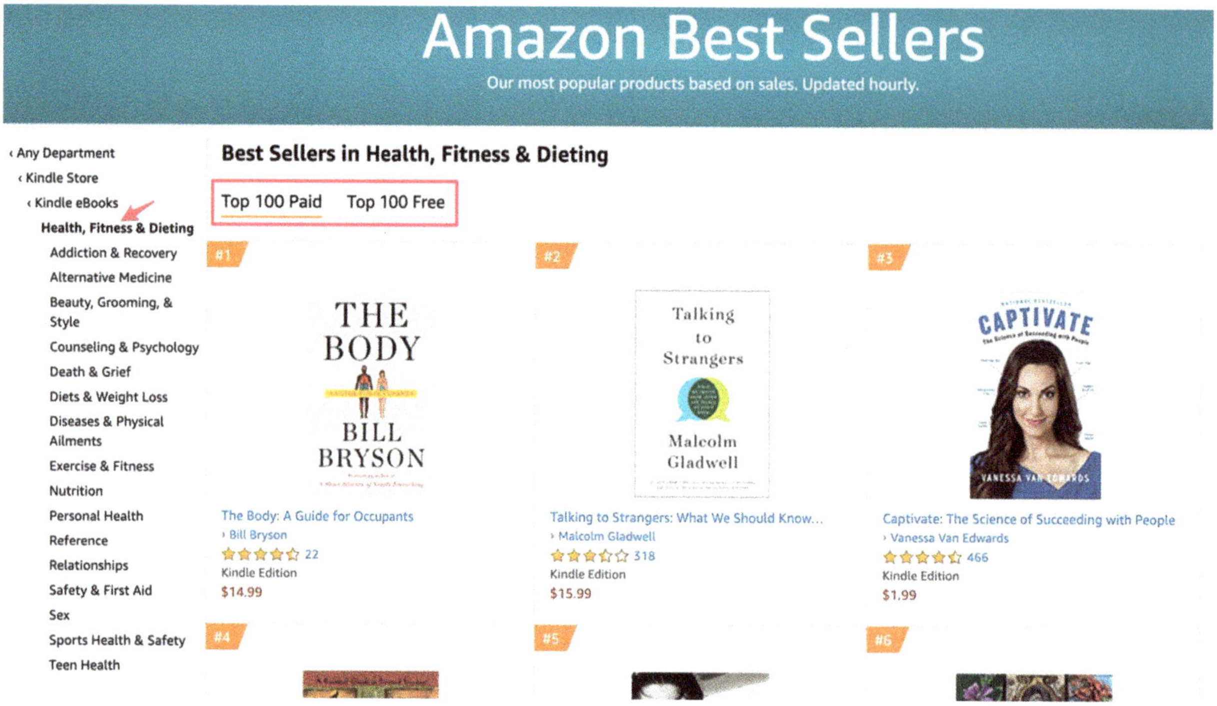

Amazon Best Sellers
Our most popular products based on sales. Updated hourly.

‹ Any Department
‹ Kindle Store
‹ Kindle eBooks
Health, Fitness & Dieting
Addiction & Recovery
Alternative Medicine
Beauty, Grooming, & Style
Counseling & Psychology
Death & Grief
Diets & Weight Loss
Diseases & Physical Ailments
Exercise & Fitness
Nutrition
Personal Health
Reference
Relationships
Safety & First Aid
Sex
Sports Health & Safety
Teen Health

Best Sellers in Health, Fitness & Dieting

Top 100 Paid   Top 100 Free

#1 THE BODY BILL BRYSON
The Body: A Guide for Occupants
› Bill Bryson
★★★★★ 22
Kindle Edition
$14.99

#2 Talking to Strangers — Malcolm Gladwell
Talking to Strangers: What We Should Know...
› Malcolm Gladwell
★★★½ 318
Kindle Edition
$15.99

#3 CAPTIVATE — VANESSA VAN EDWARDS
Captivate: The Science of Succeeding with People
› Vanessa Van Edwards
★★★★½ 466
Kindle Edition
$1.99

#4

#5

#6

在主螢幕上可以看到有兩個分類，如上圖：

- Top 100 Paid (前 100 名付費電子書排行榜)
- Top 100 Free (前 100 名免費電子書排行榜)

Top 100 Paid 是目前在這個時間點上在 Health，Fitness&Dieting 這個分類賣的最好的 100 本付費電子書，而 Top 100 Free 就是在這個分類被下載最多次的免費電子書。我們要看的是 Top 100 Paid 這部分。

我們可以瀏覽看看在這個分類大賣的都是哪些書? 有沒有哪些是我們可以參考的? 或是有興趣的? 把它們先記錄下來，比如說我對以下的書有興趣，我就先記錄起來。如下：

- The Belly Fat Diet: Lose Your Belly，Shed Excess Weight，Improve Health
- The Power of Now
- Make Him Beg To Be Your Boyfriend In 6 Simple Steps

Amazon BestSellers Top 100 (亞馬遜最佳銷售排行榜)的顯示方式是每頁 50 筆資料，如果要看到更多的書名，可以把捲軸往下拉找到其他在這個類別電子書的排名資料，如下圖：

我們可以這樣子的方法，去左側欄其他的分類看看是否有其他的書是我們有興趣的，因為這些都是大賣的書，所以你可以很放心的確認這些書的分類市場絕對是個利基市場，重點是，如果我們也出版同樣的電子書，我們的書有沒有機會大賣，這就要跟之後要說明的競爭力分析很有關係。

不過這裡有個小提醒跟大家分享，如果你找到的書是最近才上市的 (兩個月內)，那可能要稍微注意一下，因為這些剛上市的書有可能是被行銷後所以排名可以擠上前一百名，有可能之後這本書就不會是大賣的書了，所以我們要找的書，最好是在前一百名，但是出版已經有一段時間了，大約是兩至三個月，這才是我們要的參考對象。

利用雜誌找主題

我們可以到 Magazines.com 去看看有哪些主題是常常曝光在雜誌上的封面，因為那會是大家很想看的主題，而且會出現在雜誌上的一些主題，就是一般大家會遇到的問題或是在找解決方法的主題。

我們到了 Magazines.com 後會看到如下圖的畫面：

我找了一本男性健康的雜誌來看，如下：

你可以看到雜誌封面上的一些標題(紅色框框)都是可以來做電子書的主題:

- Look Awesome in 14 Seconds Flat
- Full Body Fit
- 96 Tips to Chill Out

你可以利用這種方法，再去看看別期的封面，是不是也其它的主題也可以作為參考。

為什麼可以利用雜誌來找利基市場，因為雜誌需要花錢發行，這些賣得好的雜誌一定都是有人會去買來看，所以一定有市場，不然這些雜誌社或出版社會辦不下去。

還有其他類似的網站像是

- eHow.com
- about.com
- dummies.com

都是可以去瀏覽看看有哪些是我們可以參考的主題。

到問與答網站或論壇找主題

這個方法是我自己蠻常用的方法，囚為會到問與答網站，像是 Quora.com 或 Answers.com 去找答案的人，通常有可能是在網路上找不到他們想要的答案，如果我們把他們問題的答案整理出來寫成一本電子書，應該也是會有賣點 (你也可以到雅虎知識家或依莉討論區去找找看有沒有哪寫主題是可以參考的)。

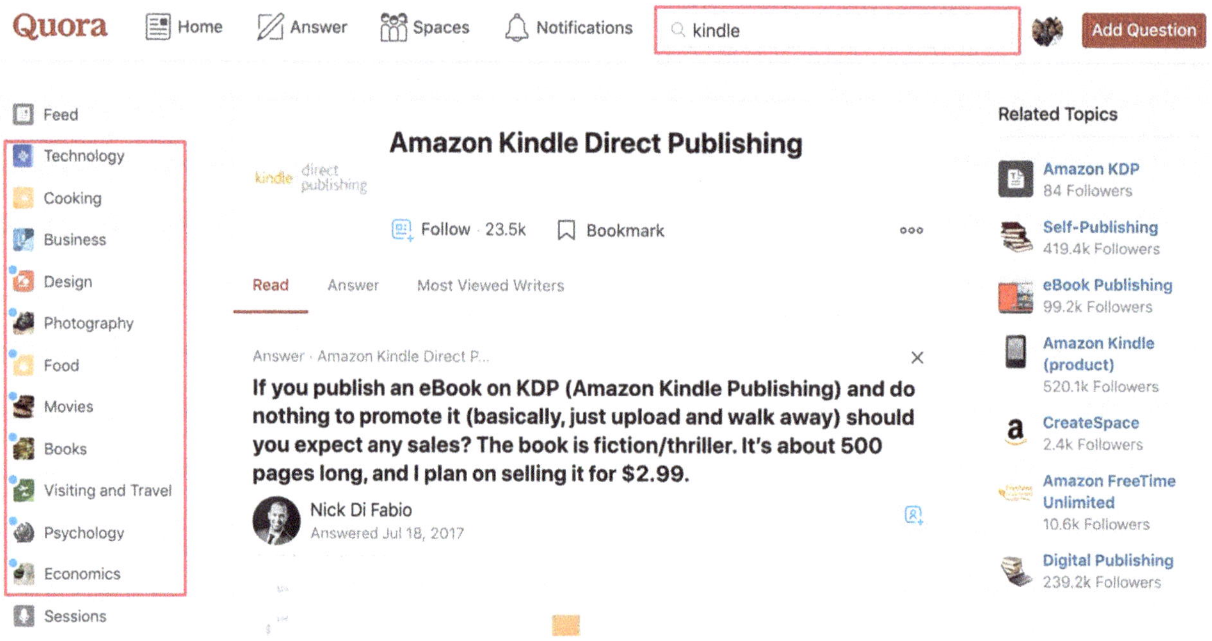

利用 Google Trends 找電子書主題

到 Google 搜尋趨勢 (Google Trends) 後，看看哪些是熱門的主題，其中左側欄裡有一個選項叫"熱門排行榜"參考看看是不是有哪些可以當成電子書的寫作主題。先把一些想法或你認為可以做的電子書主題紀錄起來。如下圖跟運動賽事有關的之類。

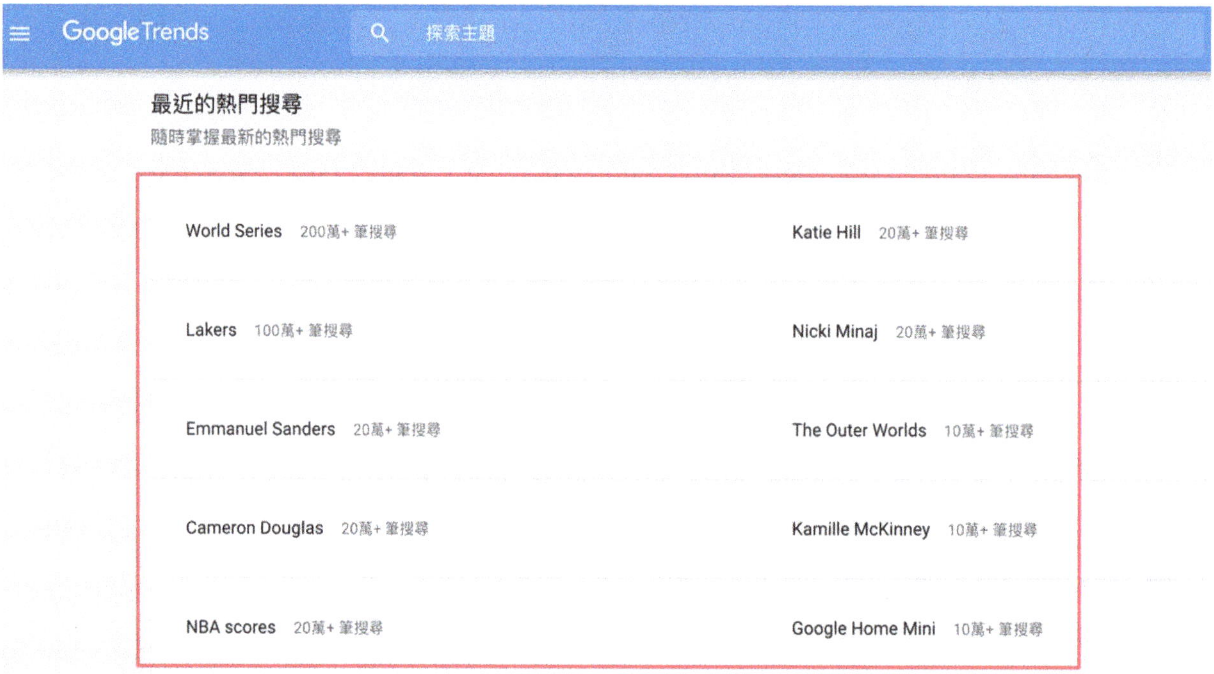

年度搜尋排行榜

查看各年份的熱門 Google 搜尋

2018 年度搜尋排行榜

2017 年度搜尋排行榜

2016 年度搜尋排行榜

2015 年度搜尋排行榜

2014 年度搜尋排行榜

利用亞馬遜搜尋引擎找主題

如果你已經有些大方向的主題後，可以利用亞馬遜的搜尋引擎來找主題，比方說我在
Amazon 搜尋列裡打上: Weight (體重)，如下圖：

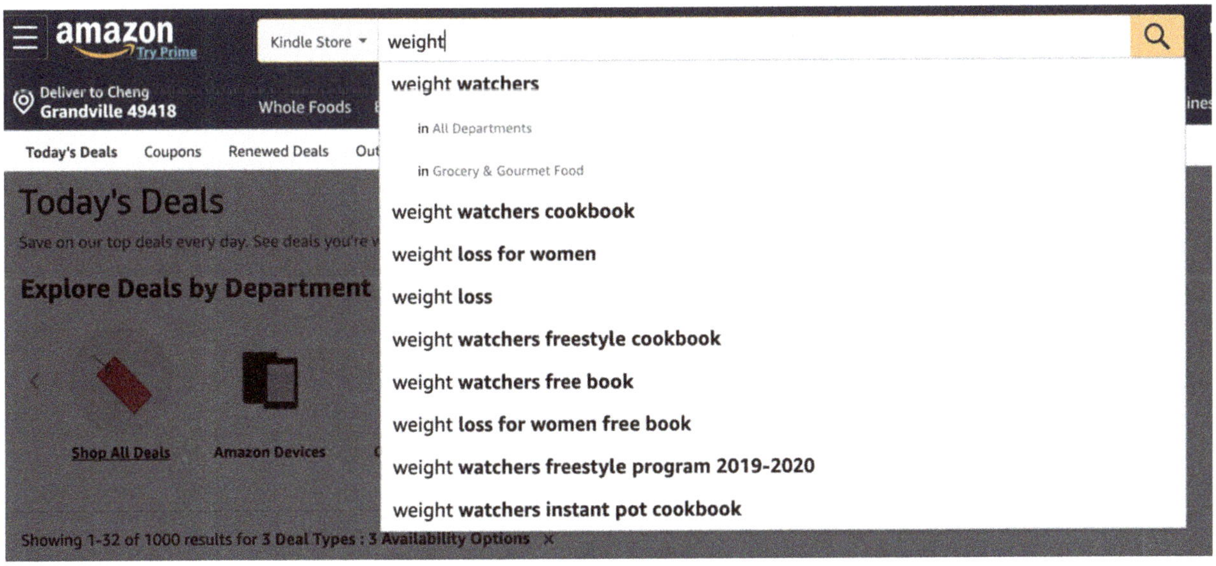

亞馬遜會自動帶出其他與 weight (體重)相關的關鍵字,如, weight loss (減重), weight watchers (體重觀測)...等等,這些出現在亞馬遜的搜尋列上,許多是消費者在找的關鍵字,我們可以利用這種方式去看看有哪些關鍵字是一般會被輸入搜尋的。

更進一步,我們可以在 weight 後面打上 a,b,c ... z,可以看出有哪些關鍵字會顯示出來

這些會出現的關鍵字有些是書名,有些則是剛剛提到消費者或瀏覽者常打的一些關鍵字,如:weight balance (體重平衡),weight control (體重控制) ...等等。利用這樣子的方式,可以去找看看有沒有適合的利基市場,比如說,我打入 weight g

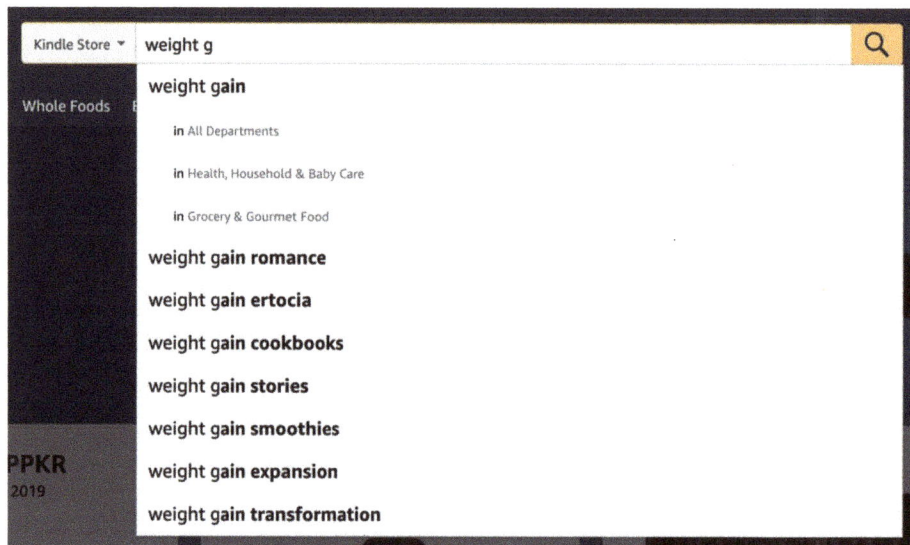

出現了 weight gain cookbooks (體重增加食譜)是我認為還不錯的關鍵字與市場,輸入 weight gain cookbooks 的關鍵字後,可以看到總共有 634 筆搜尋結果,如下圖:

只要是搜尋結果不大於 1,000 (上圖紅色圈起來的結果)，表示競爭量不大，但又有市場在，我認為都是還可以去做的市場。這裡搜尋結果的部分，我們之後在競爭力分析，會談的更詳細一些。

利用上述的六個方式我想你應該很快地可以給自己一些做電子書主題的想法，在這個階段我們只需要先把想到別人對某樣東西或做某件事情他們是覺得有趣的先記錄下來，比如說：

- Yoga (瑜伽)
- Marathon (馬拉松)
- Basketball (籃球)
- Facebook Games (Facebook 遊戲)
- How to be healthier (如何更健康)
- Speed reading (速讀)
- Increase memories (增加記憶力)
- Save money tips (省錢技巧)
- DIY PC (自己組裝電腦)
- Photography (攝影)

這些是我用上面提到的六大方法，去找到別人可能對這些主題是有興趣的，這些主題我把它們叫做大主題市場，因為這些市場有的是比較廣的，例如 (Photography) 攝影，這樣還不算是一個利基市場 (niche market)，但在這階段我們先把所有可以想到的各式各樣的大主題先把它們列下來，最好是可以列出至少 20 個大主題，當然越多好，但也不要為了一直找主題，花太多時間。

把大主題作延伸

下一步要做的就是，從這些找的大主題去做延伸，比如說 Yoga (瑜伽)，我們可以將它延伸為：

- Pregnancy yoga (懷孕瑜珈)
- Weight loss yoga (減肥瑜珈)
- Yoga for couples (雙人瑜珈)

如果想不出來，可以利用 Google Keyword planner 關鍵字工具輸入 Yoga 後，看看有沒有其他相關的主題或關鍵字是我們可以參考的，如下圖：

按下上圖的取得結果搜尋後會出現像下面的畫面：

我們可以看到，像是：Hatha Yoga (哈達瑜伽)，Bikram Yoga (熱瑜珈)，是我可以從關鍵字工具找的的主題。利用這個方式去把大主題做延伸。

利用這樣子的方式，我們應該可以找到許多有潛力的利基市場，當然這只是第一步，之後我們還要做這些利基市場的競爭力分析，這樣才能確保我們在亞馬遜電子書商城 (Amazon.com)銷售的電子書可以賣的好.

利用上述的幾種方法，將初步的電子書利基市場調查完成後，應該會有許多大主題，如下圖：

Cat caring
- Cat foods
- Cat training

Abs diet
- Weight gain diet
- Muscle building diet

101 summer games
- Summer games for kids
- Winter games for kids
- Games for kids

Raising child
- How to talk to kids
- Why kids lie

Wine
- Wine making tips
- How to make wine

我找到約 20-30 個主題。比如說: cat foods (貓食)，cat training (貓咪訓練)是比較小眾的市場，可以是利基市場，cat caring (貓咪照顧)就是比較大的市場，像 cat caring (貓咪照顧)這種主題我叫它做大主題市場關鍵字。

我們要的是延伸過後的主題，所以像是 cat foods，cat training 或是 weight gain diet (增重飲食)，muscle building diet (健身飲食)，這些才是我們要的，這些我也叫它們為利基市場，而這些關鍵字，如：Cat foods，cat training，weight gain diet，muscle building diet，就叫做，利基市場關鍵字

電子書主題競爭力分析

確定好要寫的利基市場主題後，再來要做的就是電子書主題的競爭分析，我們主要是利用亞馬遜搜尋引擎結果來做競爭力分析。甚麼是亞馬遜搜尋引擎結果？就是你在亞馬遜的搜尋列打上關鍵字後按下搜尋鈕後，所出現的結果，如下圖：

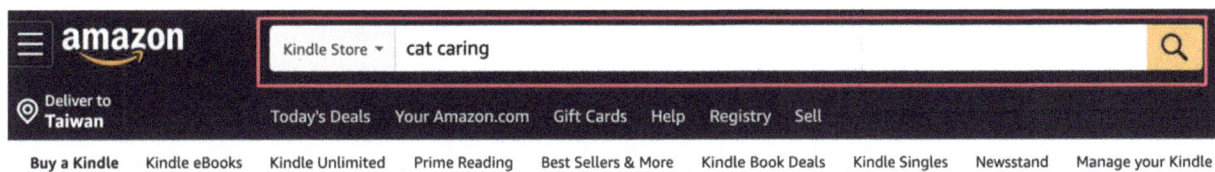

1-16 of 543 results for **Kindle Store** : "**cat caring**"

Kindle Unlimited
☐ Kindle Unlimited Eligible

Department
‹ Any Department
  Kindle Store
    Cats
    Crafts, Hobbies & Home
    Animal Care & Pets
    ⌄ See more

Avg. Customer Review
⭐⭐⭐⭐☆ & Up

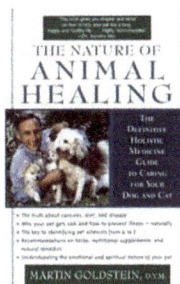

The Nature of Animal Healing: The Definitive Holistic Me
Cat
by Martin Goldstein | Sold by: Random House LLC
⭐⭐⭐⭐☆ ⌄ 365
Kindle Edition
$**13**⁹⁹ $~~17.00~~

🖱 Buy now with 1-Click ®

亞馬遜的搜尋引擎與 Google 不同,所以我們要思考的方向也會有稍許的不同,以亞馬遜電子書來說,關鍵字的分析固然重要,但個人覺得重要的程度,不會像是跟一般做網站一樣那樣重要,因為如果你是以做網站推聯盟行銷產品的話,那找到對的關鍵字 (購買意向關鍵字/buying keywords) 會非常重要。

以亞馬遜來說,電子書的書名固然重要,但更重要的是書的內容,與後面的行銷工作,目前排名在最前面幾名的都是小說類的電子書,如果你仔細看,它們並沒有所謂的關鍵字調查,比較重要的是小說的內容是否夠吸引人。若是非小說類的電子書,關鍵字是我們可以增加銷售量的一項因子,所以我們要來好好研究一下,我們可以利用主題關鍵字與下面談到的幾個方式來評斷這個利基市場在亞馬遜電子書的競爭程度。

Kindle Store 搜尋結果

在上一步中我們把有興趣主題輸入到亞馬遜搜尋列去看看有哪些書在架上賣,並且把有潛力的書名記錄下來,接下來對於這些書,我們要仔細地研究一下。

比方說我在亞馬遜搜尋引擎列裡打了 "get ex back" 這樣的主題關鍵字,結果我看到下面這樣的搜尋結果:

我們可以看到總共有 787 個搜尋結果，我們要的是搜尋結果筆數大於 100 筆，小於 1，000 筆。為什麼呢？小於 100 筆的市場可能會太小，結果會沒有甚麼人會來買這類市場的書，大於 1，000 筆的市場，對新手來說可能會太競爭，如果我們認為我們有機會在這個市場上跟別人競爭，也是可以找大於 1，000 筆的市場來做，但如果我們是剛開始的話，我建議去找符合下列條件的市場：

100 筆<主題關鍵字在 Kindle Store 的搜尋結果< 1，000 筆

這是我們做競爭分析所看的第一項因子。

接著我們繼續在這市場 (get ex back) 上看看，結果我看到了一本書: Make Him Beg To Be Your Boyfriend In 6 Simple Steps，

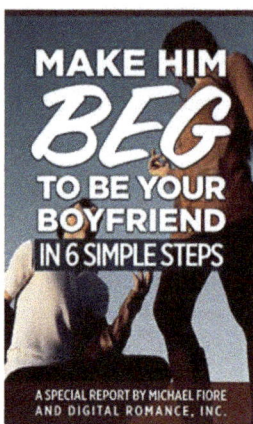

我們來看一下這本書：

封面

一本很棒的電子書封面可以為我們帶來許多優點，想想看我們去逛書局找書或其他物品的時候，一定是先看到吸引我們的畫面，我們才會繼續仔細地看，電子書的封面也是如此，一個具有吸引力的封面會為我們後面的行銷加分許多。

那怎樣的封面才是一個好的封面呢？封面這牽涉到每個人審美觀的不同，不過我認為一個可以幫助我們的書大賣的封面應該具備下面特性:

1. 封面紹的書名讓人容易理解且可一目了然

如上面範例，書名為: Make Him Beg To Be Your Boyfriend In 6 Simple Steps，讓人一看就知道這本書是男女關係有關

2. 封面與書名有相關的圖畫或照片

封面上的圖畫很容易讓人理解這是有關兩性關係的書。所以封面是我們要看的第二個因子，如果你看到這個市場也許多還不錯的封面，表示這是大家所要推廣的市場，是我們也可以考慮的一個市場。

價錢

再來我們可以點選進去看一下這本書的內容:

這本書的單價顯示為 $3.14 美金，但實際上在美國販賣只有 $2.99，會顯示$3.14 是因為我們身處美國國外，亞馬遜多收取的費用會作為電子書購買的國際傳輸下載費用與我們在台灣境外購物的消費稅。另外看到 $0.00 kindle unlimited，那是有購買亞馬遜電子書城月租服務的會員，才可以用 $0.00 購買。

一本書只賣$2.99 美金的確很有吸引力，尤其是對哪些對兩性關係有興趣的人，這也是這本書會大賣的原因，，如果這本書賣到$9.99 美金那可能就不會賣得這樣好了，所以電子書在定價上是需要好好去測試一下，看看價錢落在哪裡是可以獲取最大利益，定價的部分我們之後會談的更詳細些。

我們可以先看看在這市場上的電子書的定價為何？如果有超過一半的書的定價都是美金 $0.99 或是$2.99 的話，我們可以確認這樣是一個可行的市場。反之，如果大部分的書的是賣比較貴$6.99 或$9.99，表示這樣子的市場會比較競爭，因為會賣這麼貴的書，他們的內容與頁數一定都比較好與多。

評價

再來要注意的就是這本書的評價，你可以清楚地看到，這本書(在我記錄時)有 899 個評價，所以如果我想買這本書的話，這些評價就又大大增加了我對這本書的信心，相信它應該是一本不錯的書. 所以我們看到有越多正面評價(四顆星以上)的書，代表著有許多的人對這樣子的市場有興趣，但相對的對於我們自營出版商(self publisher)來說，要出版類似的書競爭就會比較大。

所以我們找的市場裡，最好是有些電子書的正面評價數很多，但有也些書沒有很多評價，這樣我們就有機會在這樣的市場上去跟別人競爭。

書的頁數

這本範例的書大約有 30 頁，一般來說，我們要做的電子書希望能控制在 150 頁以下，原因是為了要控制成本，我們的書會是專注在國外市場，如果英文不是很好的話，會希望是外包電子書的寫作， (我所有上架的書全數是外包)，頁數越多，代表我們要花的成本越多，如果要寫到 200 頁以上，這樣花費不但多，要是最後書沒有大賣，要把成本賺回來就相當困難。

低成本有一個好處，有可能在電子書上架後的一到二個月就可以把成本賺回來，一般來說，我所做的書外包成本剛開始都設定大約是$50 美金一本(現在大約需要$150-$200 美金)，一本大約 30-50 頁，字數大約在 12，000-25，000 字左右。(不過這只是參考值，許多時候要看寫手的能力與評價為何? 如果寫手是美國人或是英語系國家的人，我給的費用會稍微高一下，如果是菲律賓或其他非英語系國家的人，就會給的少一點，這個可以自己去拿捏一下。)

目前我架上的書 (大約有 500 本書)成本約在美金$10-$800 的範圍內，我的結論是，便宜的成本如$10 或$20 美金並不一定會賺不到錢，而$800 美金的書也不一定就會大賣，因為後面的行銷與書是否吸引人才關鍵，當然重點是書的品質不能太爛，原則上，想要好品質的書，外包的單價一定會稍微高一些，但是為了成本考量，我建議新手外包一本書最高最高不要超過$250 美金。(目前我每本書的外包成本大約都抓在$150-$200 之間，都是英語系國家的寫手)

書的銷售排名

以剛剛的例子來看，再把捲軸往下，你可以看到 Product Details 的部分，裡頭會有這本書的銷售排行，如下圖:

Product details

File Size: 124 KB
Print Length: 30 pages
Publisher: Digital Romance Inc; 1 edition (June 1, 2012)
Publication Date: June 1, 2012
Sold by: Amazon Digital Services LLC
Language: English
ASIN: B00887JUQC
Text-to-Speech: Enabled ☑
X-Ray: Enabled ☑
Word Wise: Enabled
Lending: Not Enabled
Screen Reader: Supported ☑
Enhanced Typesetting: Enabled ☑
Amazon Best Sellers Rank: #14,911 Paid in Kindle Store (See Top 100 Paid in Kindle Store)
#39 in Love & Romance (Kindle Store)
#3 in 45-Minute Self-Help Short Reads
#2 in 45-Minute Parenting & Relationships Short Reads

這本書在我寫這本電子書時，在所有目前幾百多萬本 Kindle 電子書中，排名是#14，911 名，表示這本書賣的相當好，給大家一個概念，排名與實際銷售數量的關係如下：

書本銷售排名	每個月大約銷售量
1-10	30，000-50，000+
100-500	10，000-30，000
500-1，000	3，000-6，000
1，000-3，000	1，000-3，000
5，000-10，000	450-600
10，000-30，000	100-300
30，000-50，000	50-100

50，000-100，000	10-20

上表的排名與銷售比只是個參考，以這個表格來估算，這本書大約每個月可以賣到 100-300 本左右，我們前面有稍微提到，在亞馬遜上架的電子書最多佣金可以拿到 70%　(亞馬遜給你七成的佣金，如果你書的賣價是介於$2.99~$9.99 美金)，如果我們以最低一個月賣出 100 本來計算，這本書的佣金約是 2.99 x 70% = 約 $2 美金，這本書每個月可以賺到約

- $2 x 100 本 = $200 美金

$200 美金的佣金，也就是相當於每個月賺台幣 6，000 元以上....(OMG...我的天啊，這本書到現在已經出版 7 年了)，光靠一本電子書每個月就可以有這樣的被動收入，這還不包含亞馬遜提供電子書租借 Kindle Edition Normalized Pages (KENP) Read (KENP)的服務。

附註：甚麼是亞馬遜電子書租借(KENP) 的服務？

在亞馬遜上的消費者如果有加入 Amazon Prime (亞馬遜的一種會員服務) 的消費者，Amazon Prime 提供一項 KOLL(Kindle Owners' Lending Library)與 KU(Kindle Unlimited)的服務，這些參加 Amazon Prime 的亞馬遜會員可免費租借有參加 KDP Select (KDP 精選) 計畫的電子書，如果我們的電子書有加入 KDP 精選計畫，只要我們的書被借出去並且被閱讀一頁，平均亞馬遜給我們約每頁$0.0045 美金的佣金。

這給我們的啟示是，這個兩性關係的市場是一個相當好的利基市場，但是我可能不會做一本跟這本書一模一樣的書，因為它的評價太多，排名太高，要擊敗它，不太容易，所以我會選擇跟它類似的利基市場，但選用不同的關鍵字來作為我的書名。

相關電子書排名

再來我們要看的是在這個主題市場相關電子書的排名，如果你打上一個關鍵字或主題到亞馬遜的搜尋列上去看看結果，亞馬遜總共會在第一頁的結果選項裡提供 16 筆的選項(這個數字有可能隨著亞馬遜搜尋機制調整而改變)，如下圖：

我們要看的是在這 16 筆電子書的排名為何？我們希望找到的是在這 16 筆電子書裡有些書的排名是好的，而我們也希望找到有些書的排名是比較差的。為什麼要這樣？原因是在這樣的主題市場裡，有些書的排名好，表示這個市場有消費者願意在這市場花錢，而有排名不好的，表示我們書的排名有機會可以超越它們，也許可以在這樣子的市場裡賣的好。

新手的相關電子書排名數據可以設定為：

- 200k <相關電子書排名< 100k

如我在"Get ex back"這個市場裡有找到下面的電子書，有些排名是< 100k，有些則是> 200k：

Product Details

File Size: 391 KB
Print Length: 47 pages
Simultaneous Device Usage: Unlimited
Sold by: Amazon Digital Services, Inc.
Language: English
ASIN: B009D0JLT4
Text-to-Speech: Enabled
X-Ray: Not Enabled
Lending: Not Enabled

< 100k

Amazon Best Sellers Rank: #28,787 Paid in Kindle Store (See Top 100 Paid in Kindle Store)
  #15 in Kindle Store > Kindle eBooks > Nonfiction > Parenting & Relationships > Family Relationships > **Divorce**
  #38 in Books > Parenting & Relationships > Family Relationships > **Divorce**

Product Details

File Size: 135 KB
Print Length: 30 pages
Sold by: Amazon Digital Services, Inc.
Language: English
ASIN: B005JU9BJ2
Text-to-Speech: Enabled
X-Ray: Not Enabled
Lending: Not Enabled

> 200k

Amazon Best Sellers Rank: #325,602 Paid in Kindle Store (See Top 100 Paid in Kindle Store)

這邊提到的數據只是給大家做一個參考，並不一定要照著這些排名數據為依據，如果你已經是老手，你也可以把這些數據標準設的更嚴格一點。比如說：

- 100k <相關電子書排名<50k

利基市場關鍵字在 Google 關鍵字工具裡的搜尋量

還有一項我們可以參考來做為我們是否要在某個市場做電子書的指標，那就是 Google 關鍵字工具裡的搜尋量，搜尋量太小，表示這樣子的市場是沒有人會去太捧場的市場，如果找出來的搜尋量小於 1，000 (1k) 筆的話，我可能就會換一個主題試試看。

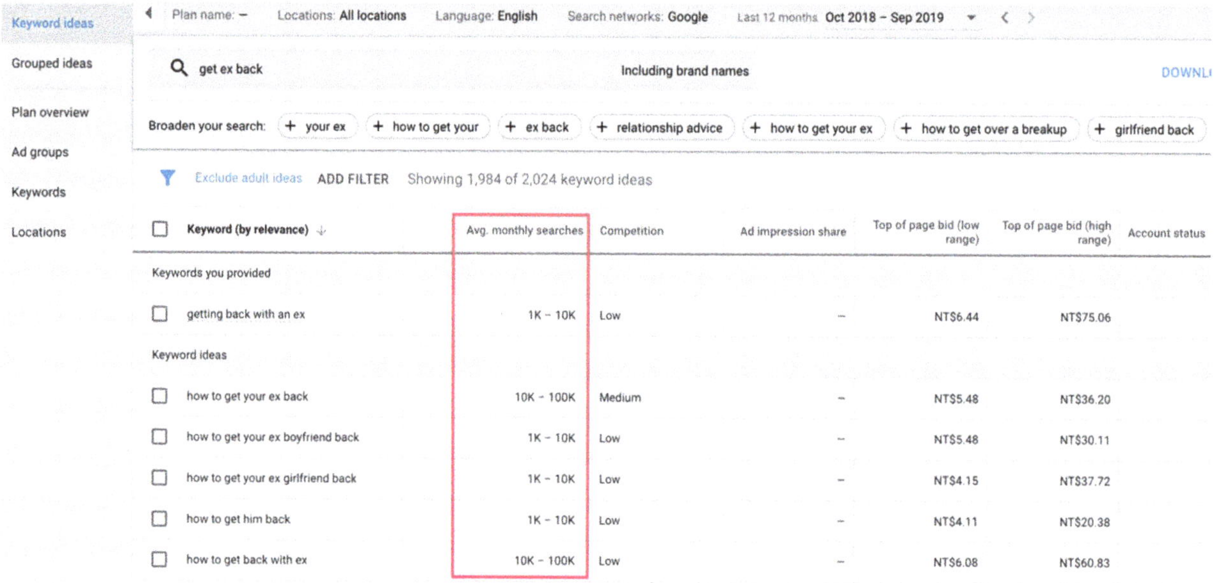

你可以看到上圖，how to get ex back 這樣子的市場全球搜尋量有 10k – 100k 筆表示這符合我們設的條件。(現在 Google 關鍵字工具需要實際執行廣告預算才會有更詳細的搜尋筆數顯示出來)

Google 搜尋透視 (Google Insights) 趨勢

我們要看的最後一項競爭分析因子就是這個市場的趨勢，要知道某個市場的趨勢是往上或往下，可以利用 Google 搜尋透視 (Google Insights)來查看：

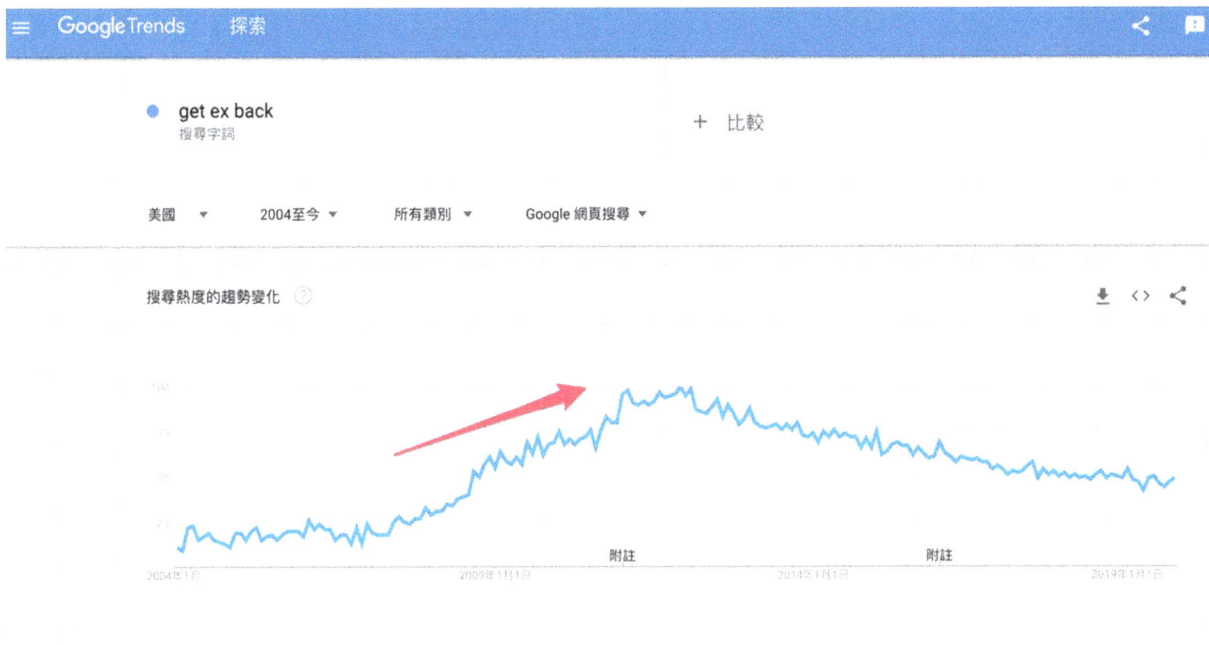

輸入主題關鍵字(get ex back)按下搜尋後，我們可以看到這個市場的趨勢為何，只要是往上或持平都是可以做的市場。

要確認某個主題適不適合來寫電子書，我們把重點整理如下：

1. Kindle Store 搜尋結果：大於 1,000 筆，小於 100 筆

2. 相關電子書頁數：小於 150 頁

3. 相關電子書排名：有< 100k，也有> 200k 的

4. 利基市場關鍵字在 Google 關鍵字工具裡的搜尋量：至少>1,000 筆

5. Google 搜尋透視 (Google Insights) 趨勢：持平或往上

如果你找的主題大部分都符合上述的條件，就可以蠻確定這樣的利基市場是可以做的。

讀者通常在買書時會注意哪些事項是對我們出版商來說要特別注意的，整體來說，書名，作者，目錄(內容大綱)，價格，封面等都很重要，而書的價值(Value)，也就是書的內容是不是能夠被消費者買單(是否能解決他們的問題或提供他們娛樂)是最重要的一項因素。

所以你在出版電子書的時候，你一定要時時刻刻記得，我們要提供給消費者的內容價值，一定要遠遠大過於消費者願意付出的價格，我們的書才會賣得好，就像是前面提到的三大步驟中的核心思想，你一定要在你的利基市場做這兩件事：

- 如何幫助更多的人
- 如何提供價值

無論是你的內容，封面還是你的行銷策略，都要把這兩點牢記在心。

如果心裡只想著要賺錢，這樣子做出來的電子書，肯定不會賣得好，其實任何東西的是一樣，就像我在寫這本電子書的經驗分享時，我要一直提醒我自己，我要提供更好更多高品質的內容給我的消費者，而且價值一定要遠遠大過於賣價，如果你在這本書沒學到任何東西，你一定要記得這個觀念。

市場建議

在做利基市場調查的時候，有一點需要注意一下，這本書或這個市場的持久性為何？是不是為長青市場(Evergreen)，舉例來說，有兩本書，一本是如何使用 Facebook，另一本是如何自然受孕，可以看出來如何受孕這本書是比較長青的市場，因為 Facebook 的介面可能常常變換，是不是時間久了如果沒有更新，大家自然就不會去買這樣的書，因為已經過時了。

也就是說也許過 1-2 年後，這本書就不賣了，而另一本書如何自然受孕卻是有可能 10-20 年後還可以繼續賣，這就是我們要做的市場，但有時候非長青市場也是可以賺到不少佣金，這就要自己去衡量了，我自己的比例大概是 80%長青市場的書，20%非長青市場的書。

再來我們來看一下哪些是 Kindle 比較熱賣的書，Kindle eBooks (Kindle 電子書) 內主要分成兩大類的書籍;

- Fiction (小說)

- Nonfiction (非小說)

如果我們仔細地去看看，我們會發現，大部分賣的比較好的書都是小說類的書，如果你對小說有興趣，可以往這方面著手以下幾類是賣的比較好的小說類別;

- [Romance](愛情浪漫類)
- [Science Fiction](科幻小說)
- [Mystery & Thrillers](恐怖疑雲)
- [Erotica](煽情類)

近期有一類的小說賣得非常好，他是由一個遊戲衍生而來的叫做: Minecraft Diary，如果你在亞馬遜上打上 Minecraft Diary，你就可以知道那是怎樣的小說了。

而我自己目前電子書或實體書的所有收入來源大約是一半小說一半非小說，因為非小說類的電子書是比較好上手的，但小說類的似乎收入有越來越高的趨勢。

我們來看看有哪些內容對新手來說是比較好上手的，以下我列了 10 大利基市場給大家參考：

參考工具書...

- [寶寶姓名參考書]
- [程式設計參考書]
- 軟硬體使用手冊，如:
    - [The Unofficial Guide to Using Evernote with David Allen's System]

點子書

點子書也是另一個新手很容易上手做的電子書，如:

- 101 個理想作方法
- 25 堂人生必修課

- 21 件人生最後悔的事

- 100 個聖誕節禮物點子

我們可以自己去 Yahoo! Answers (雅虎知識＋) 或其他相關論壇蒐集一下資料，然後可以很快地自己創作或是外包請寫手幫我們把這些點子書寫好，不過可以到哪裡去找點子呢? 像上面的例子都是我在書局的雜誌區或是 Facebook 上面看到的，到書局到處看看或去 Facebook 上看看，其實可以得到許多的啟示與想法，有些就可以把它做成點子書。

還有另一個方法可以找點子書的主題，在 Kindle Store 搜尋列上打上數字，如 100 或 101，我們可以看到有許多的點子書都是我們可以參考的:

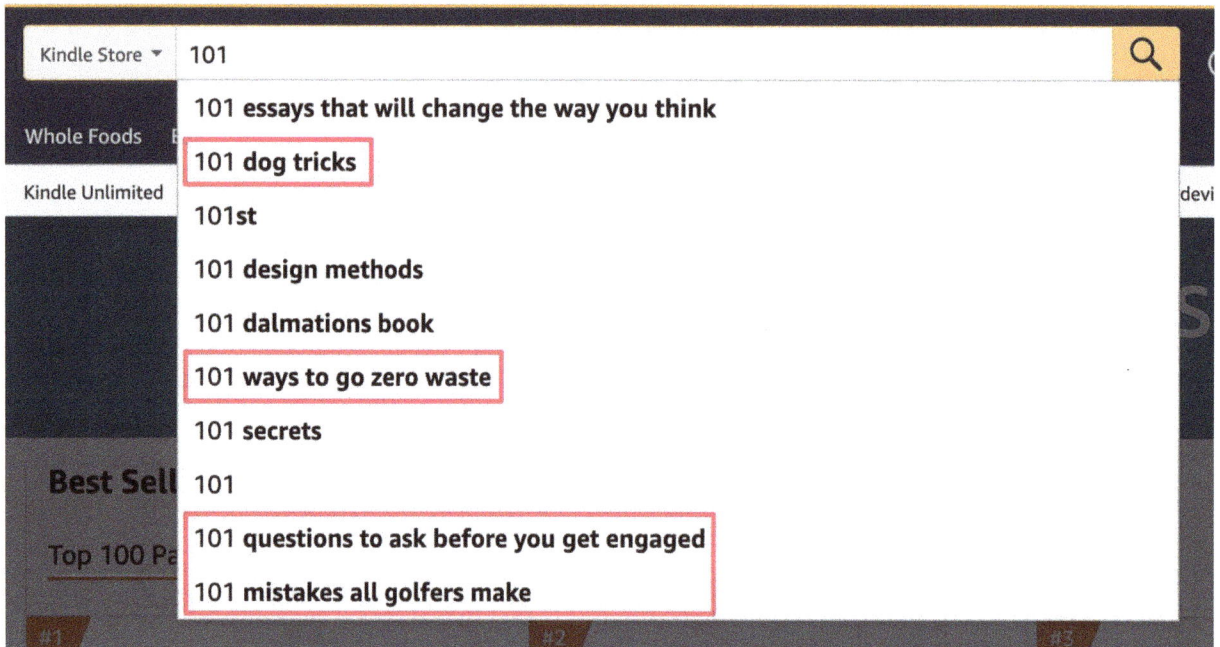

下面是在亞馬遜上賣的一些例子

- [101 Conversation Starters for Couples](#)
- [101 Good Questions to Ask on a Date](#)
- [50 Romantic Date Ideas](#)
- [101 Knock Knock Jokes for Kids](#)
- [88 Great Daddy-Daughter Dates](#)

- [81 Overlooked and Undervalued Ways to Save Money](#)

開箱文 (非長青)

像是有一些我們可以常常在 [mobile01.com](#) 看到的電子產品開箱文，都可以把它寫成電子書，有些也是賣得相當好，只是這類的書是非長青市場，要自己去衡量看看。

- [iPhone 11 Series USER GUIDE](#)
- [All-New Fire HD 8 & 10 User Guide - Newbie to Expert in 2 Hours!](#)

找工作類

教人家如何找到工作，如何應付面試等等都是還不錯的市場。

- [Job Interview Questions & Answers: Your Guide to Winning in Job Interviews](#)
- [101 Great Answers to the Toughest Interview Questions: Sixth Edition](#)

小孩類

小孩類的書也很好做，但是競爭大一些，要爭取到好的排名較不容易，但是一個可以嘗試的市場。

- 字母學習書
- 顏色數字認知書
- 故事書
- [動物認知](#)

自我學習類

自我學習有太多方面可以去找市場，這是一個還不錯的市場。

- Time management (時間管理)
- Goal setting (目標設定)

- Survival Guide (economic collapse and natural disaster) (天災妨害)

關係類

- 如何約會，男女關係這是一個很好的市場。
- Dating (約會)
- Get ex back (關係複合)

健康類

不外乎就是一些大家常見的健康方面的需求之類的主題

- Weight loss (減肥)
- Build muscle (健身)
- Organic living (有機生活)
- Natural health (天然的健康)

如何....類電子書 (How to guide)

如下圖，你可以利用 how to a ， how to b ， ... how to z，的方式，把英文字母打上搜尋列去看看出現哪些主題或有哪些書是可以參考的。這個也是我蠻常用的方法找市場。

Kindle Store ▾ | how to a|　🔍

how to a**nalyze people**

how to a**ttract men**

how to a**nalyze people free book**

how to a**bsurd scientific advice for common real-world problems**

how to a**nalyze people the ultimate guide**

how to a**ttract men free book**

how to a**nswer interview questions**

how to a**merican**

how to a**void falling in love with a jerk**

how to a**rgue and win every time**

Whole Foods

ŋ-sung
2009

season

Kindle Store ▾ | how to b　　🔍

how to b**e an antiracist**

how to b**uild the best habits**

how to b**e an anti racist**

how to b**e a good creature**

how to b**e funny**

how to b**e yourself**

how to b**abysit a grandma**

how to b**ang a billionaire**

how to b**e a family**

how to b**eguile a duke**

Whole Foods

ŋ-sung
2009

season

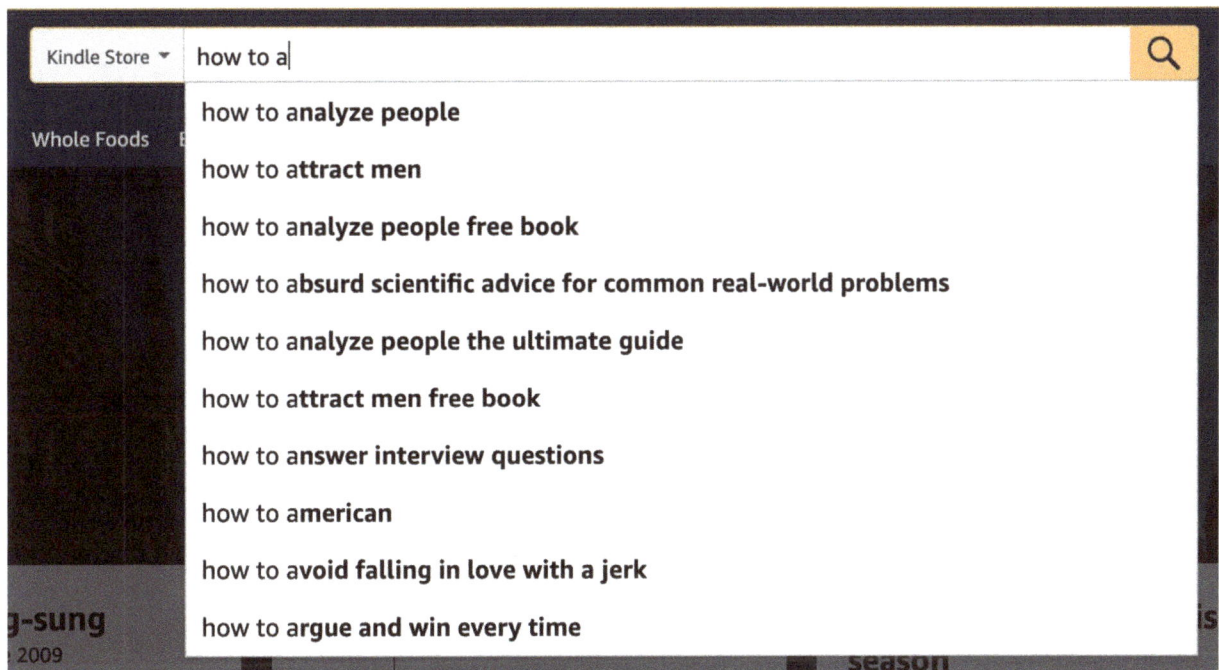

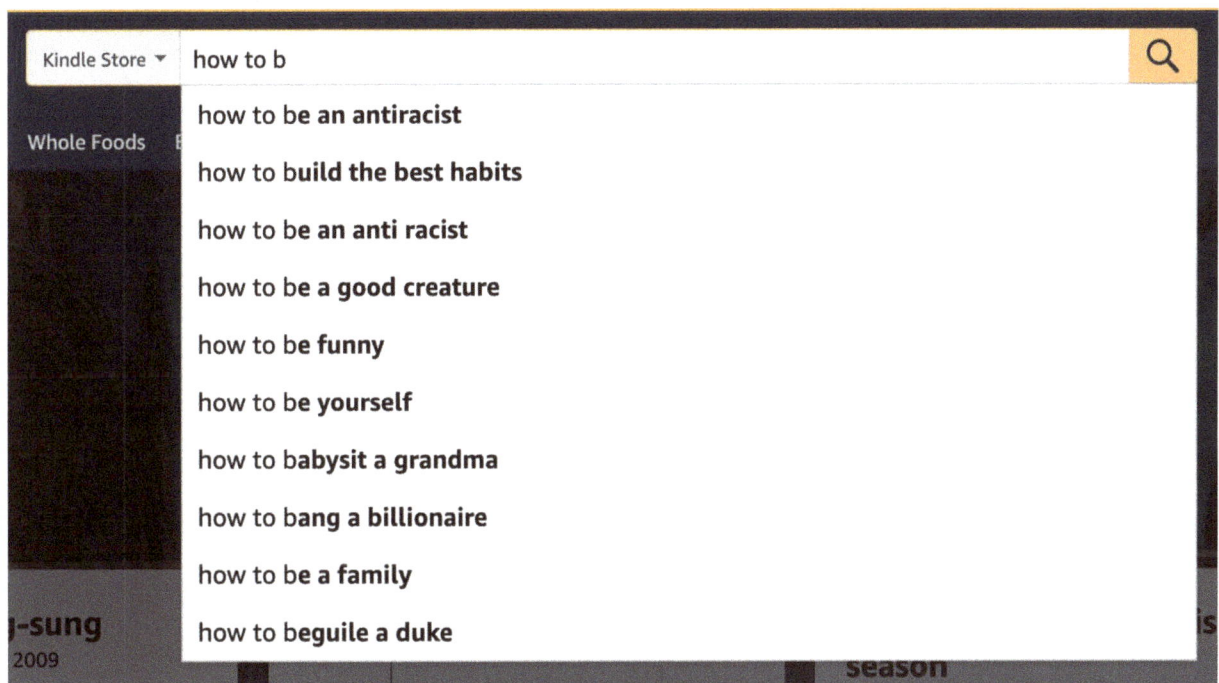

利用這種方式我找到如：

- How to draw (如何畫圖)

- How to attract women/men (如何吸引異性)

- How to be happy (如何快樂)

這些都是可以當成電子書主題的一些方向。

你可以看到我們花了相當多的時間在市場調查上面，這是因為利基市場的選擇是最重要的，我們的電子書能不能大賣跟你選的主題有相當大的關係，所以我們要花最多的時間在這。確定好主題後，下一步我們要做的就是針對我們選擇的主題，我們要寫甚麼樣的內容。

第 2 步: 內容創建 - 寫什麼內容?

內容大綱製作(TOC)

確定好要做的主題後，就可以開始著手寫書，但是要寫怎麼樣的內容才會吸引人呢? 有幾個方法可以嘗試一下:

到問與答的網站找資料

我最常用的方法就是到 Yahoo Answers!(中文的是雅虎知識家)或是跟我們想要做的利基市場的相關論壇或討論區去找大家都在問什麼？然後把這些問題蒐集起來後，整理成一份內容大綱後，自己寫作或交給外包寫手去發揮，這是我自己最常用的一個方法。

把前面提到的主題關鍵字打到 Yahoo Answers 裡去看看有哪些問題是很多人在問的，把它們選起來，當作你內容大綱的一部分，如下圖我以"Bengal Cats"作為我的主題關鍵字：

Keeping a bengal hybrid cat??

Hi there... Bengal cats are a lot more physically active than domestic cats...common suggestion for anyone interested to have a Bengal cat is that this particular breed isn't a good cat...

3 Answers · Pets · 12/03/2012

Bengal Cats?

Hi Rachel... Bengal cats "CAN" be great house pets, however.... 22 pounds is not common for a Bengal cat unless they are overweight which presents...

2 Answers · Pets · 28/07/2008

Adopting a Bengal Cat ?

Bengal cats love water. If they don't like to get into it...the adult bengal is already used to domestic cats. Bengals are a dominate breed, I have seen with...

7 Answers · Pets · 25/08/2011

Who has a Bengal kitten/cat?

Bengals are wonderful cats - but they're NOT for everyone... a day, or vacation often, a Bengal is NOT for you. These cats need a lot of attention, and left alone...

4 Answers · Pets · 29/08/2008

Anyone one know about Bengal cats?

Hi there...Bengal cats "CAN" be great house pets, however...the outdoor enjoyment. In some regions the Bengal cat is outlawed as a pet so be sure to check...

8 Answers · Pets · 17/05/2008

Does anyone know anybody with a bengal cat?

I do own a Bengal cat, and have recently written an article...a *lot* of research before buying a Bengal. They are extremely beautiful cats, but they are NOT for everyone...

4 Answers · Pets · 08/05/2008

看到我覺得還不錯的問題，就先把它複製起來，整理起來。

參考其他本類似主題電子書的內容大綱

到 Kindle Store 到搜尋列上打上主題關鍵字，找到類似的書後，按"Click to LOOK INSIDE"，

就可以看到其他書的內容大綱，

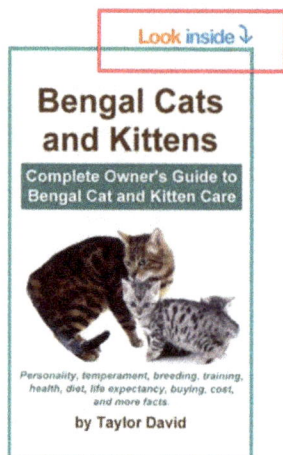

Bengal Cats and Kittens: Complete Owner's Guide to Bengal Cat and Kitten Care Kindle Edition

by Taylor David ˅ (Author)

⭐⭐⭐⭐☆ ˅   36 ratings

› See all 8 formats and editions

Kindle	Paperback
$0.00 kindleunlimited	$12.99

Read with Kindle Unlimited to also enjoy access to over 1 million more titles
$5.03 to buy

18 Used from $3.10
7 New from $12.99

Everything you wanted to know about bengal cats and kittens. Guaranteed to answer all your questions, this book is a must for anyone passionate about Bengals.

Personality, temperament, breeding, training, health, diet, life expectancy, buying, cost, and more facts.

Table of Contents

可以參考這些大綱作為你自己的大綱，但千萬不要完全照抄，如果你完全照抄，很有可能會被亞馬遜把你的帳號整個關掉。

到相關論壇去找資料

可以在 Google 搜尋列上打上"主題關鍵字+forum"，如："Bengal cats forums"，找到相關的論題或討論區後，看大家在論壇裡都在問什麼樣的問題，把這些問題記錄起來，作為你電子書內容大綱的一部分

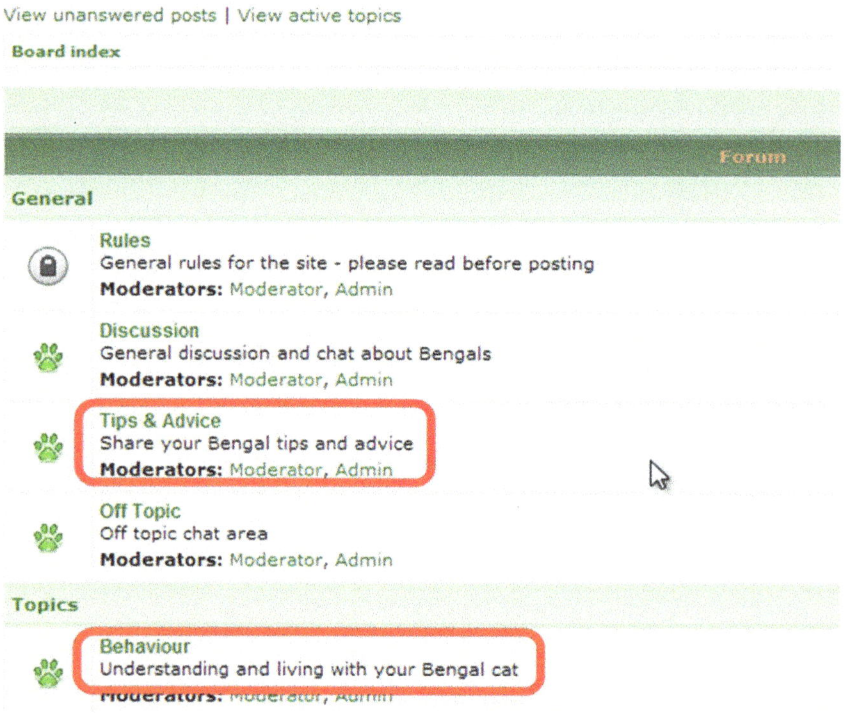

View unanswered posts | View active topics

Board index

Forum

General

🔒 **Rules**
General rules for the site - please read before posting
Moderators: Moderator, Admin

🐾 **Discussion**
General discussion and chat about Bengals
Moderators: Moderator, Admin

🐾 **Tips & Advice**
Share your Bengal tips and advice
Moderators: Moderator, Admin

🐾 **Off Topic**
Off topic chat area
Moderators: Moderator, Admin

Topics

🐾 **Behaviour**
Understanding and living with your Bengal cat
Moderators: Moderator, Admin

利用上述的方法找好相關的問題與資訊後，整理好內容大綱 (TOC)後，也就是我們電子書要寫的內容會像是下圖這樣：

你可以看到我把相關的重點或問題整理在同一個章節 (Chapters)，大部分我會至少整理 5-7 個章節，每個章節 5-7 個重點來做為我電子書的內容大綱。

附註：在製作內容大綱時也會花不少時間，如果你不想自己製作，也可以將這部份外包。

內容寫作

好了，假設我們已經有做好的內容大綱 (TOC) 在手上了，下一步就是要怎麼寫電子書，千萬記得我們在做電子書，質比量重要，所以不要亂寫，或用 PLR 的書去上架，因為如果品質不好或是有太多瑕疵，書可能會被亞馬遜下架，甚至你的帳號會被停權，永遠無法使用。

附註：甚麼是 PLR

PLR 英文是 Private Label Right，也就是擁有私訂標籤的權利，意思就是說某些文章，電子書或任何形式的產品，如果是宣告有 PLR 的權利，你可以對這些文章或產品做任何的修改與處理，要說作者或擁有者是你自己也可以，你擁有百分之一百的權利對這些 PLR 做任何事，包含出售或轉售。

但我們要做的書都是英文書，除非你的英文還不錯，或是你喜歡寫作，不然我建議將<u>內容寫作</u>的這部分，外包給專業的寫手來創作。國外有許多的專業寫手 (ghostwriter) 他們是以寫作維生，花點錢交給這些寫手，會給你自己省下非常多的時間。

一般來說，我會比較建議把電子書外包給專業的寫手來創作，也許你本身英文夠好，或許你喜歡寫作，但是要自己寫出一本還不錯的書是要花相當的時間，我會建議外包是因為，我們可以把時間省下來做更有效的利用，比如說，學習更多的賺錢知識或是與家人相處，我自己目前所有的書都是外包，外包的平台我自己比較喜歡使用的有下列幾個：

- Upwork.com
- Guru.com

其他還有許多平台可以使用像是 freelancer.com ， iwriter.com 或是 epicwrite.com，我自己最常用的則是 Upwork.com。這些平台大多都有第三方保護的功能，你先把錢利用 Paypal 或是信用卡匯到這些平台，等寫手給你內容文件後，我們滿意後再付款。

另外一些方式去看看有哪些書是中文的，你覺得還不錯，可以自己看過讀過後，簡單地把它寫成英文(如果你英文夠好的話)，然後再給外包寫手潤稿。

應徵寫手範例

在這邊，我提供一個簡單的應徵寫手範例給大家參考：

這是應徵<u>英文電子書寫手</u>的工作職缺範例，紅色的部分請改成你想要做的電子書主題以及需求條件， 例如我想做的主題是跟慢跑(Jogging)有關，紅色的部分就把它改成我的主題，如: Jogging

發表職缺流程如下：

到 Jobs(錄用)後，於 Enter the name of your job post，輸入工作職缺，如：Jogging Writers Needed!

下一步則在 Job Category，選擇一項適合你的寫作職缺，如：Ghostwriting 後，點擊 Next 繼續。

進入頁面後，於 Description 處輸入工作職缺內容。

Description

A good description includes:

- What the deliverable is
- Type of freelancer or agency you're looking for
- Anything unique about the project or team

輸入工作職缺內容

Are you jogging person? If you do and know how to write your experience，you might be the one we are looking for.

We want to hire someone who can write a topic about jogging. This is an easy job if you are already a jogging person.

If you think you can do this，please reply back with your bid. To let us know that you have read the job description，put "jogging" as your first word in the first sentence.

2258/5000 characters (minimum 50)

Additional project files (optional)

drag or upload project images

You may attach up to 5 files under **100 MB** each

Back | Next

這裡提供一份工作職缺範例如下，這只是給你參考用，記得要把紅色部分改成你要做的主題，藍色的部分為給寫手寫作的天數一般設為 **10-14** 天即可 請自由調整內容，不要完全一樣，避免外包帳號被鎖。

如有需要上傳相關的檔案，最多 **5** 個檔案，檔案總大小 **100mb** 以下；如沒有問題，可點擊 Next 繼續。

應徵寫手工作範例:

Are you jogging person? If you do and know how to write your experience，you might be the one we are looking for.

We want to hire someone who can write a topic about jogging. This is an easy job if you are already a jogging person.

If you think you can do this , please reply back with your bid. To let us know that you have read the job description , put "*jogging*" as your first word in the first sentence.

IMPORTANT!!!

This is REALLY IMPORTANT!! WE DO NOT ALLOW PLAGIARISM! You can't just copy content from internet and paste as your work. We will check for your work , all materials must be original and unique content. If your work is found to be plagiarized , we will report to proper authorities and we will NOT pay for it!

A signed contract stating that this is a WORK FOR HIRE creation that you will own NO rights to and that your name will appear nowhere on or within and that I will own all rights to including resell and distribution rights.

THE REPORT MUST BE DELIVERED IN:

- A font size of 12 points

- Times new roman font type

- Single spaced between all breaks (chapters , subtitles...etc)

- With margins no more than 1" on all sides (left , right , to , bottom)

- You don't need to create a TOC (Table of Content) , we'll supply our reference Outline/TOC to you

- The report has to have at least 50 pages , which is around *15k-20k*words. (images/reference links are not counted as a page)

- We also need a separate Microsoft Word file for 2-3 paragraphs talking about what this report is about , kind of like sales pitch talking to potential readers why they should read this report , kind of poke their problems and mention this report will provide them solutions.

We are aiming to get the completed project to be delivered in Microsoft word within *10-14* days after we have a contract.

Again , I am looking for a writer to work with long term on a variety of topics as long as your content is of quality and your price per report is reasonable.

This is a VERY EASY writing job for some people (not all writers could do this) , so please bid fairly.

Reply back with your first sentence saying: ' *jogging* ' with your previous samples or any of your work , so that we know you've read through this description and you're serious.

Thanks.

再來選擇外包專案的性質，這邊分為三種：

- One-time project (一次性的工作)

- Ongoing project (持續性的工作)

- Complex project (大型且複雜的工作)

一般來說，選擇一次性的工作性質 (One-time project)即可，之後點選 Next 繼續。

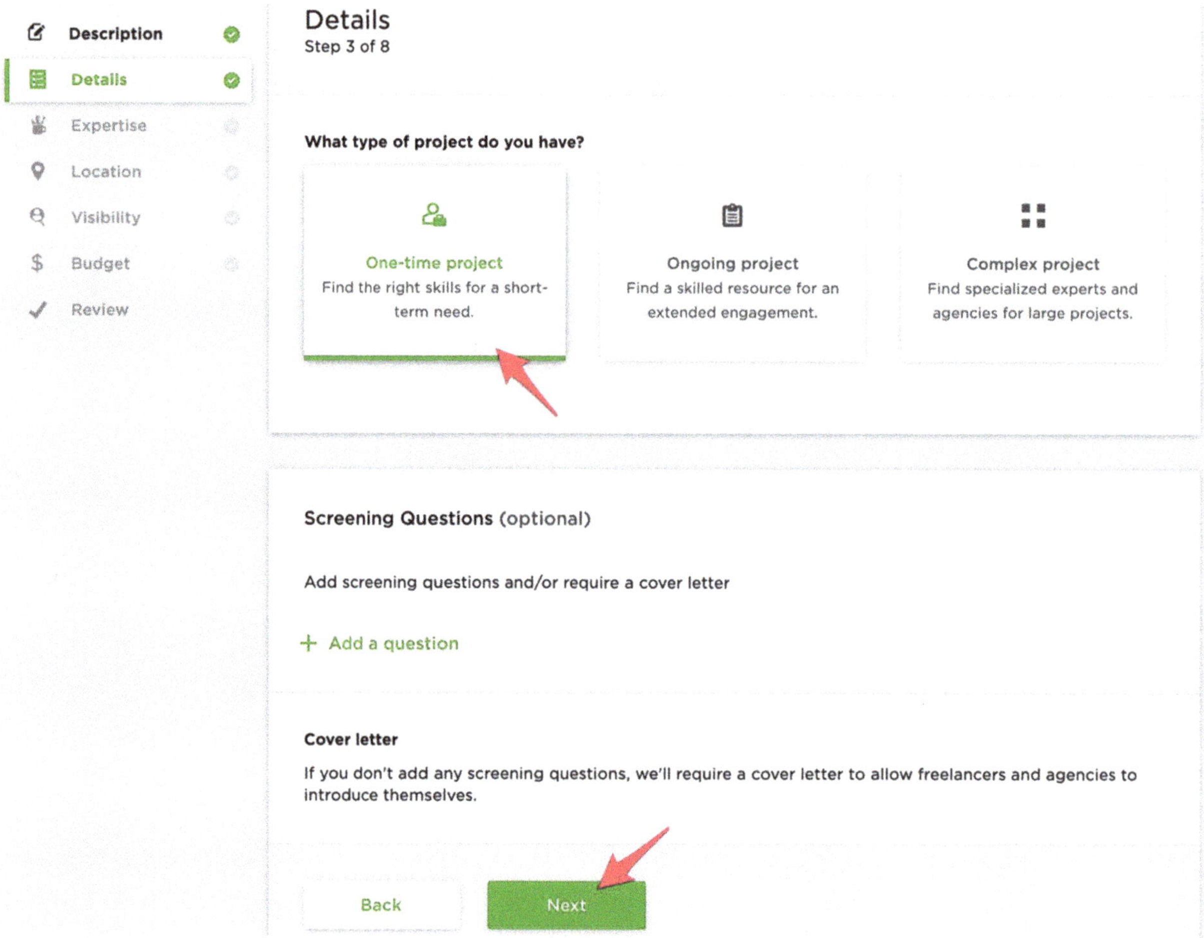

在接下來的一步主要是點選這份工作職缺所需要的技能裡，點選你認為勝任這份工作所需即可，點選後技能會變成綠底白字，如下圖：

Expertise
Step 4 of 8

What skills and expertise are most important to you in Ghostwriting?

Ghostwriting Services (optional)

Ghostwriting   Editing & Proofreading   Fact Checking   Research   See more

Ghostwriting Deliverables (optional)

Autobiography   Biography   Blog Content   Article   Novel   eBook   See more

Written Languages (optional)

English   French   German   Spanish   Arabic   Chinese   See more

What additional skills and expertise are important to you?

Writing   Content Writing   Creative Writing   English Grammar   PHP   Internet Research

Article Writing   Web Design   Ghostwriting   WordPress   Website Development   Blog Writing

CSS   HTML5   JavaScript   HTML   SEO Writing   Copywriting   Data Entry   CSS3

Not what you're looking for?

Type to add a different skill

Back   Next

確定後再點擊 Next 繼續。

選擇你想找的人住在哪裡，在這個範例裡，我選擇只要找住在美國的寫手，來幫我完成寫手的工作，確定後選擇 Next 繼續。

Visibility
Step 6 of 8

Who can see your job?

Anyone
Freelancers and agencies using Upwork and public search engines can find this job.
任何人都可看到我的工作職缺

Only Upwork talent
Only Upwork users can find this job.
只有在Upwork的人才可以看到我的工作職缺

Invite-only
Only freelancers and agencies you have invited can find this job.
私密的工作職缺

How many freelancers do you need for this job?

One freelancer
只錄用一人

More than one freelancer
錄用多人

再來是你工作職缺的曝光度，我想讓越多人看到越好，我選擇 Anyone，並且只錄用 1 人就選 One freelancer。

再來選擇寫手的背景，一般來說這些選項都預設即可，只有英文程度 (English Level) 我會選擇最好，也就是流利或母語是英文的人 (Native or Bilingual only)。

Talent Preferences (optional)

Specify the qualifications you're looking for in a successful proposal.

Freelancers and agencies may still apply if they do not meet your preferences, but they will be clearly notified that they are at a disadvantage.

Talent Type

No preference ⌄

Job Success Score ❓

◉ Any job success
○ 80% & up
○ 90% & up
☑ Include Rising Talent ❓

Amount Earned

◉ Any amount earned
○ $100+ earned
○ $1k+ earned
○ $10k+ earned

English Level

○ Any level
○ Conversational or better
○ Fluent or better
◉ Native or Bilingual only

+ Add other languages

Group

No preference ⌄

Back   Next

再來是 **Budget** 的部分，選擇固定薪制後，填上你想要外包的金額，一般我都填上$50 左右，如果沒有人來應徵，可以再改成多一點如：$100 美金。其他部分不用更改，再按綠色按鈕 Next 繼續。

Budget
Step 7 of 8

How would you like to pay your freelancer or agency?

POPULAR

Pay by the hour
Popular for ongoing projects

Pay a fixed price
Popular for one-time projects

時薪制   固定薪制

Do you have a specific budget?

$ 50

What level of experience should your freelancer have?

$
Entry

$ $
Intermediate

$ $ $
Expert

Back   Next

最後瀏覽整份工作職缺，如果沒有問題，點擊 Post Job Now，即完成工作職缺發佈。

upwork   JOBS   FREELANCERS   REPORTS   MESSAGES   Q ∨ Find Freelancers   ? 🔔 👥 👤

Title ✓
Description ✓
Details ✓
Expertise ✓
Location ✓
Visibility ✓
Budget ✓
✓ Review

Review and post   Post Job Now

Title   ✏

Title
Jogging Writers Needed!

Job Category
Ghostwriting

內容確認 (Copyscape)

如果我們成功地收到外包寫手的電子書文件後，第一步要做的就是檢查這本書的內容是否有抄襲的部分，我們可以將文件的內容全部複製後，貼到 copyscape 裡去看看有哪些部分是有抄襲嫌疑的。

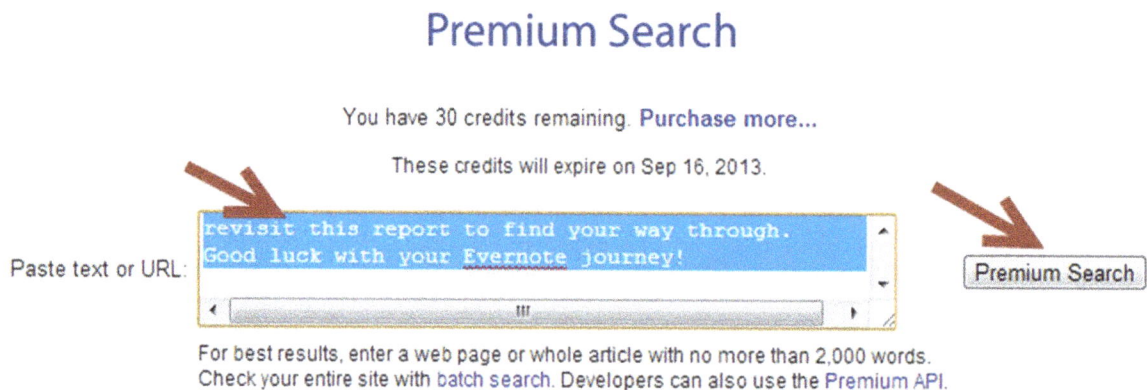

copyscape 是一個網路服務，它可以自動地去檢查出文件的內容有多少是跟網路上的資料重複的。如果外包寫手遞交的文件有抄襲的話，就必須要求寫手重新寫作或重新雇用新的寫手，如果有抄襲的文章內容的話 copyscape 會幫我們抓出來如下圖：

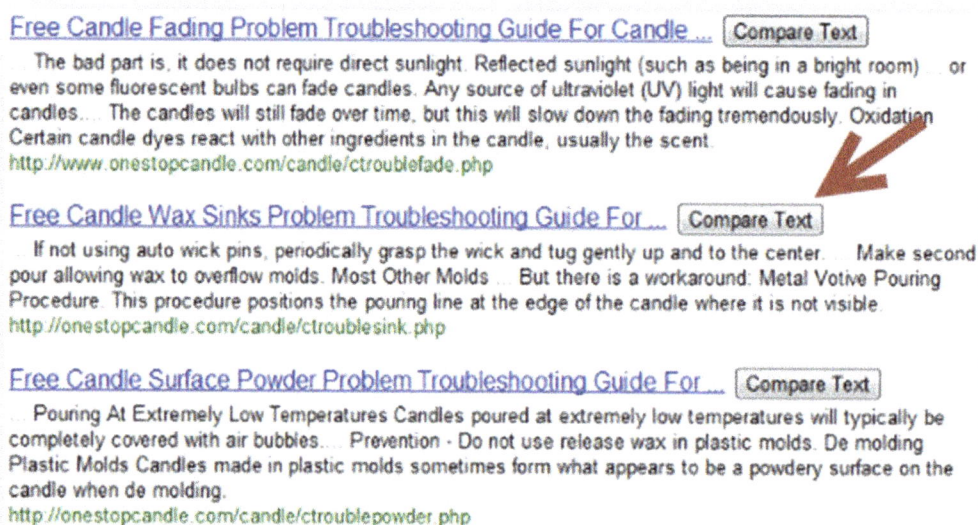

按下 Compare Text 就可以知道這份文件有多少內容是有抄襲的嫌疑了，一般來說除了是引用別人的話，基本上用 copyscape 檢查時，是不應該出現任何有抄襲嫌移的畫面才對，如果沒有任何抄襲的部分，就可以到下一步去做電子書檔案的編輯，準備上架。

Copyscape 是需要付費的服務，如果你不想花錢，可以把寫手的作品一段一段話貼到 Google 去搜尋看有沒有相關或一模一樣的文字，如果有就很有可能是抄襲的。

電子書製作

確認書名

內容確定無誤後，首先要做的就是確認電子書的書名，因為我主要是做非小說市場的電子書，在大部分的情況下，電子書的書名或是我們選的利基市場關鍵字會影響電子書本身在亞馬遜搜尋引擎上的排名，雖然說書名不是絕對決定排名的唯一因素，但還是有其重要性在，所以我們要盡量把我們想要的利基市場關鍵字，讓它出現在電子書的書名上，這很重要，舉例來說: 我在亞馬遜的搜尋列上選擇 Kindle Store 後，打上 superfoods，這個關鍵字，我們來看一下出現的第一本書如下圖:

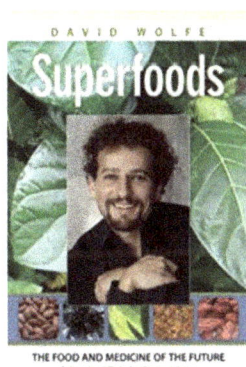

Superfoods: The Food and Medicine of the Future
by David Wolfe | Sold by: Penguin Random House Publisher Services
★★★★☆ ˅ 363

Kindle Edition
$13⁹⁹ $18.95

Buy now with 1-Click ®

它的書名叫做:

Superfoods: The Food and Medicine of the Future

書名的第一個字就是 Superfoods 這樣的主題關鍵字，所以你可以知道，讓關鍵字出現在書名上的重要，但是千萬也不要過度使用，如果可能的話，至少使用兩次是我自己覺得還不錯的模式。

其他書名的命名方式可以去參考相關書籍的書名名稱，比如說找到其他賣的比較好(排名盡量在 50,000 以內)類似的書 4-5 本，去觀察這些書的書名有哪些相類似的關鍵字，我們也可以把它們記錄起來，應用在我們自己的電子書上。

檔案編輯

在這一步裡，我們主要要做的文件檔案編輯有下列幾項：

- 加入作者名 (Author)
- 加入版權宣告
- 拼字檢查
- 利用 Word 自動建立目錄 (Table of Content)
- 製作電子書壓縮檔

加入作者與版權宣告

你可以選擇一個筆名來做為你電子書的作者名，因為目前電子書最大的市場在美國，所以我會取比較美式的筆名來做為我電子書的作者名，如果你想不出來有甚麼美國名字可以取的，可以去 Google 搜尋"Most popular American names" (最常見的美國名字)，就應該可以有一些主意了。或是你可以到以下這些網址去看看有哪些名字是你可以用的。

http://www.fakenamegenerator.com/

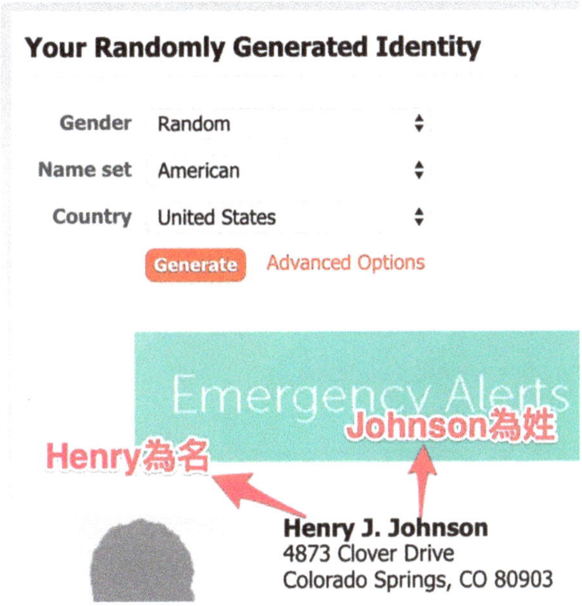

Your Randomly Generated Identity

Gender	Random	⇕
Name set	American	⇕
Country	United States	⇕

Generate Advanced Options

Emergency Alerts

Henry為名   Johnson為姓

Henry J. Johnson
4873 Clover Drive
Colorado Springs, CO 80903

http://www.lifesmith.com/comnames.html

如下圖第一張圖是前 50 大美國名字的姓，第二張是前 25 大男性與女性的名。

50 Most Common American Surnames (US Census 1990)

1. Smith	11. Anderson	21. Clark	31. Wright	41. Mitchell
2. Johnson	12. Thomas	22. Rodriguez	32. Lopez	42. Perez
3. Williams	13. Jackson	23. Lewis	33. Hill	43. Roberts
4. Jones	14. White	24. Lee	34. Scott	44. Turner
5. Brown	15. Harris	25. Walker	35. Green	45. Phillips
6. Davis	16. Martin	26. Hall	36. Adams	46. Campbell
7. Miller	17. Thompson	27. Allen	37. Baker	47. Parker
8. Wilson	18. Garcia	28. Young	38. Gonzalez	48. Evans
9. Moore	19. Martinez	29. Hernandez	39. Nelson	49. Edwards
10. Taylor	20. Robinson	30. King	40. Carter	50. Collins

25 Most Popular American Male Names
25 Most Popular American Female Names

1. James	11. Christopher	21. Ronald	1. Mary	11. Lisa	21. Michelle
2. John	12. Daniel	22. Anthony	2. Patricia	12. Nancy	22. Laura
3. Robert	13. Paul	23. Kevin	3. Linda	13. Karen	23. Sarah
4. Michael	14. Mark	24. Jason	4. Barbara	14. Betty	24. Kimberly
5. William	15. Donald	25. Jeff	5. Elizabeth	15. Helen	25. Deborah
6. David	16. George		6. Jennifer	16. Sandra	
7. Richard	17. Kenneth		7. Maria	17. Donna	
8. Charles	18. Steven		8. Susan	18. Carol	
9. Joseph	19. Edward		9. Margaret	19. Ruth	
10. Thomas	20. Brian		10. Dorothy	20. Sharon	

比如說我找一個女性名為 Mary，姓為 Smith，我的筆名就可以是：Mary Smith。

版權宣告

再來就是要加入電子書的版權宣告意思就是說版權所有，翻印必究的意思。最簡單的方式，就是加入以下文字敘述：

All rights reserved.

No part of this publication may be copied , reproduced in any format , by any means , electronic or otherwise , without prior consent from the copyright owner and publisher of this book.

Disclaimer

The information contained in this ebook is for general information purposes only. The information is provided by the authors and while we endeavor to keep the information up to date and correct , we make no representations or warranties of any kind , express or implied , about the completeness , accuracy , reliability , suitability or availability with respect to the ebook or the information , products , services , or related graphics contained in the ebook for any purpose. Any reliance you place on such information is therefore strictly at your own risk.

完成作者與版權宣告後，文件會看起來像下圖一樣：

Bug Out Bag

How to Make the Ultimate Bug-Out Bag

Robert Reinoehl

PUBLISHED BY:
Robert Reinoehl
Copyright © 2013

All rights reserved.

No part of this publication may be copied, reproduced in any format, by any means, electronic or otherwise, without prior consent from the copyright owner and publisher of this book.

Disclaimer

The information contained in this ebook is for general information purposes only. The information is provided by the authors and while we endeavor to keep the information up to date and correct, we make no representations or warranties of any kind, express or implied, about the completeness, accuracy, reliability, suitability or availability with respect to the ebook or the information, products, services, or related graphics contained in the ebook for any purpose. Any reliance you place on such information is therefore strictly at your own risk.

以下有一個英文作者範本給大家參考，範本中紅色的部分是自己要做修改的，中文請自行上 Google 查詢即可：

- http://goo.gl/yIeuCB

拼字檢查

雖然拼字檢查是很基本的，但是還是有許多時候寫手再交給你文件的時候，會沒有做到這點，所以我們要在利用 Word 的自動拼字檢查再做一次檢查。無論是英文或中文的內容，都應該仔細校稿後再上架。

利用 Word 自動建立目錄

接下來我們要做的是利用 Microsoft Word 裡的自動建立目錄(TOC)功能，將目錄建立起來.詳細流程可參考上面連結 (但我們要把頁數的選項剔除掉，因為電子書沒有頁數的問題，頁數會根據讀者的閱讀器與閱讀字型大小設定有關，所以目錄不像實體書一樣需要頁碼)。

整個流程大致如下：

先將在文件內看看有哪些文字是要顯示在目錄上的，通常是章節的部分，選起來後，再去選擇標題的樣式，如下圖：

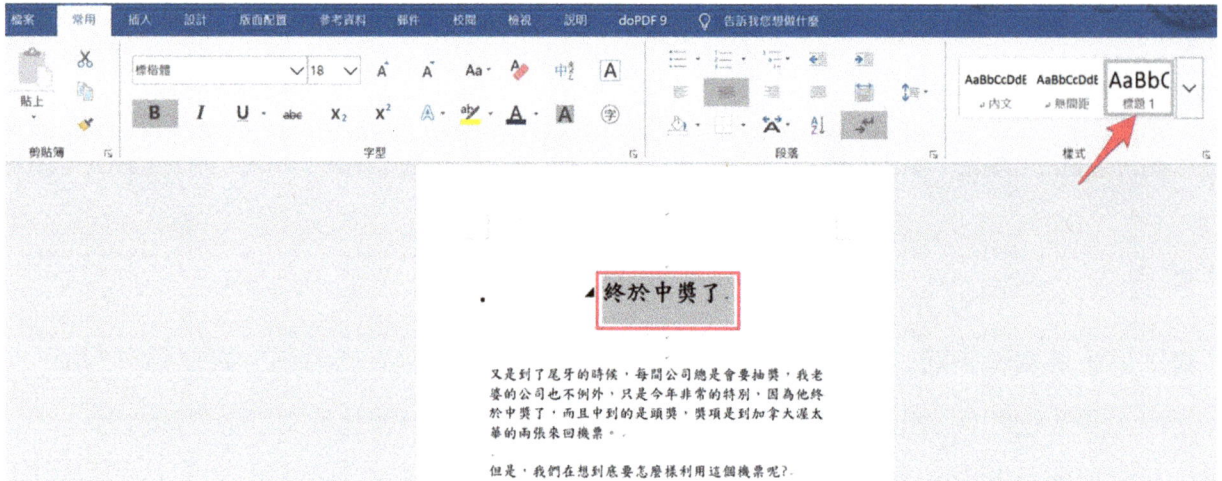

全部的章節的選擇好後，再點選參考資料 > 目錄 > 自訂目錄，如下圖：

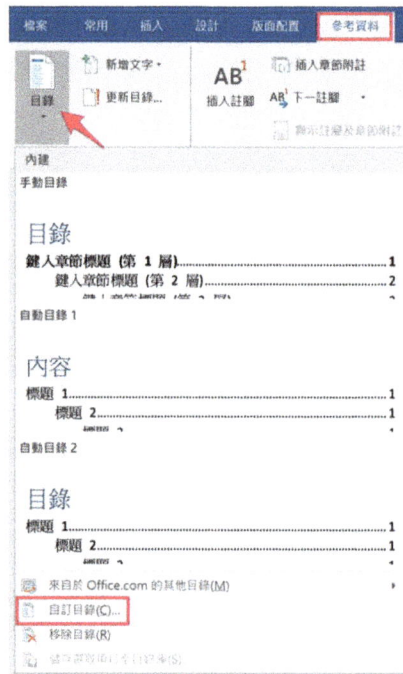

再來記得不要勾選顯示頁碼，因為亞馬遜電子書是不支援頁數的，按下確定鈕就完成了。

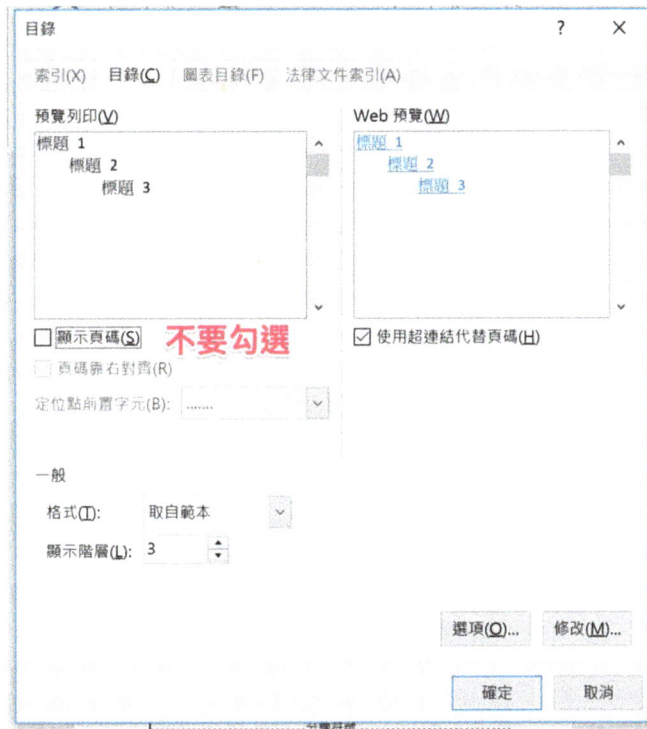

我們可以從下圖看到已經利用 Word 的自動建立目錄功能，把電子書的目錄做好了。

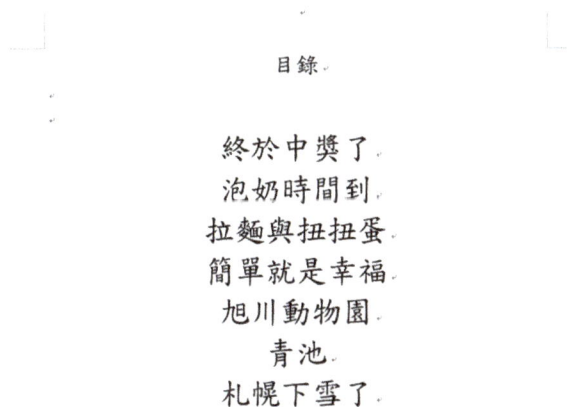

接下來就是把檔案儲存，整本書在儲存 Word 格式時目錄就會自動完成了。

要這樣做的目的是因為亞馬遜電子書是以網頁的方式來表現，我們利用 Word 的自動建立目錄功能能讓我們不需要會寫網頁，就可以很快地把具備有網頁連結 (anchor) 的電子書做好。

感謝所有家人

分頁符號

目錄

終於中獎了
泡奶時間到
拉麵與扭扭蛋
簡單就是幸福
旭川動物園
青池
札幌下雪了

分欄符號

終於中獎了

具備有這樣功能的電子書，也才會讓瀏覽者閱讀起來更方便。

圖片

上面提到，有些書會有圖片或照片，如果你想要增加頁數或是電子書的可看性，可以到以下幾的地方加入一些跟我們電子書有相關的圖片，但是記得所用的圖片是要沒有版權的問題喔！

- https://pixabay.com/
- http://www.wikipedia.org/
- http://search.creativecommons.org/

使用這些圖片最好是在圖片下方聲明圖片來源，因為亞馬遜非常重視版權的問題，宣告我們的圖片來源可以避免掉不必要的麻煩，如下圖:

Image by Nacho y Adriana on Flickr under Creative Commons license

Image by Nacho y Adriana on Flickr under Creative Commons License

封面製作

內容完成後，接下來要做的就是書本的封面，之前談到一個好的封面可以為我們的書帶來多點收益，如果我們自己的美工 okay 的話，可以用 paint.net 自行去設計封面，或是到 Fiverr 打上 Kindle cover 外包封面，

以下是幾個我認為比較好的封面

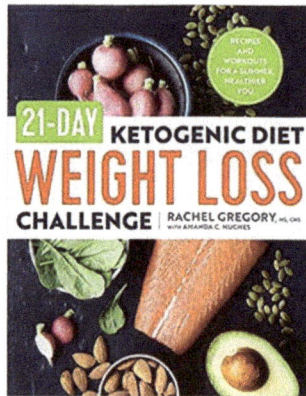

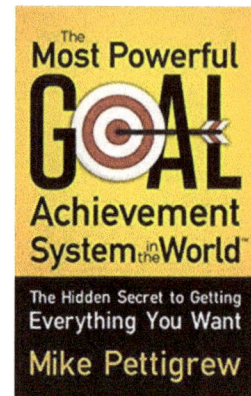

封面設計要項

記得，對我們個人電子書出版商來說，一個好的封面要有

- 書名讓人容易理解且可一目了然
- 封面與書名有相關的圖畫或照片
- 封面底色盡量不要用白色
- 色彩有強烈的對比，如黑底白字或淺色底深色字體，讓書名可以跳脫出來

還有記得 Amazon 上面有封面的規格，長寬比為 1.6:1，但是我會建議把封面大小設計成 2，700 x 1，800 像素(pixels)，因為到時候如果你要把你的電子書轉換成實體書，大部分的實體書尺寸都是 6"x9"，而且要 300dpi，換算下來就是 2，700 x 1，800 像素(pixels)。

第 3 步: 上架行銷 - 去哪賣電子書?

申請 KDP 帳號

如果你還沒有亞馬遜的任何帳號，首先要做的就是去申請亞馬遜 KDP 電子書出版平台的帳號，如果你已經有亞馬遜的任何帳號的話，你可以直接用舊的帳號，以下跟大家說明如何去申請 KDP 的帳號

打開瀏覽器後，在網址列上輸入 http://kdp.amazon.com

之後我們會看到下列畫面，如果你從來都沒有註冊過亞馬遜帳號，請點選 Sign Up，如果你已經有註冊過亞馬遜帳號，要點選 Sign In 後，亞馬遜會要求你輸入 email，在這裡可以通用，直接輸入你的亞馬遜 email 與密碼就可以了，

如果你是新用戶，還沒有使用過亞馬遜任何服務，請選擇建立您的 KDP 帳號(Create your KDP account)灰色按鈕，

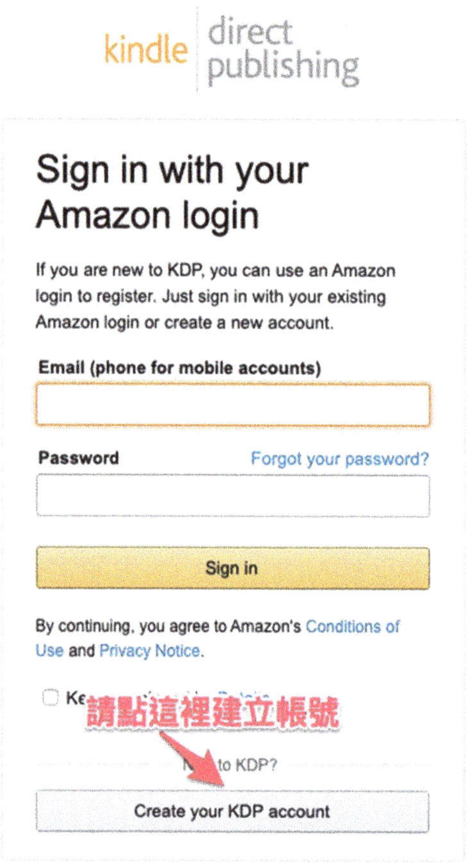

kindle | direct publishing

Sign in with your Amazon login

If you are new to KDP, you can use an Amazon login to register. Just sign in with your existing Amazon login or create a new account.

Email (phone for mobile accounts)

Password   Forgot your password?

Sign in

By continuing, you agree to Amazon's Conditions of Use and Privacy Notice.

請點這裡建立帳號

New to KDP?

Create your KDP account

亞馬遜會要求你註冊帳號，輸入如下圖的資訊後：

Create account

Your name

| 輸入你的英文名字

Email

輸入你的email

Password

At 輸入密碼(至少6位字元)

i Passwords must be at least 6 characters.

Re-enter password

再次輸入密碼

Create your KDP account

By creating an account, you agree to Amazon's Conditions of Use and Privacy Notice.

再點選 Create your KDP account(建立帳號)的黃菊色按鈕後，若出現以下畫面，則是亞馬遜需要你先到 email 開信，找到亞馬遜給你的一次性密碼(OTP)，輸入後再點擊 Create your KDP account 按鈕，

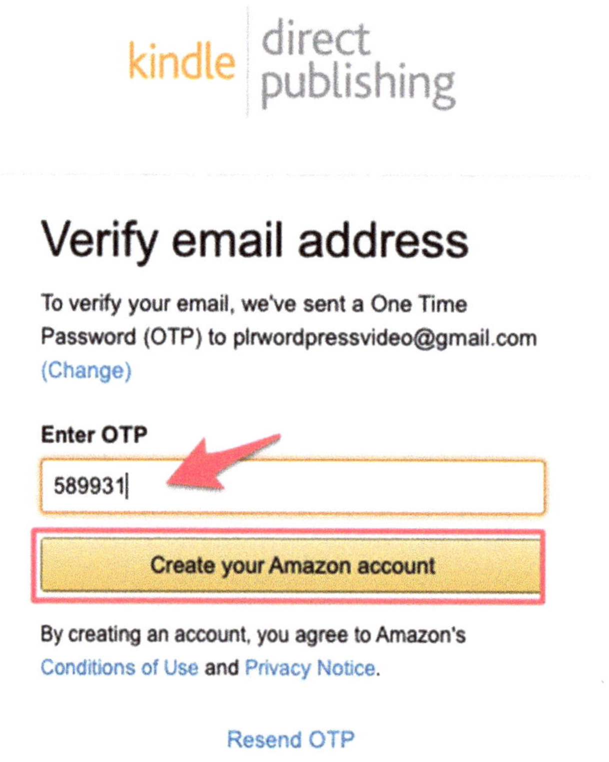

kindle direct publishing
Verify email address
To verify your email, we've sent a One Time Password (OTP) to plrwordpressvideo@gmail.com
(Change)
Enter OTP
589931
Create your Amazon account
By creating an account, you agree to Amazon's Conditions of Use and Privacy Notice.
Resend OTP

之後將進入 KDP 網站使用暨註冊同意條款如下圖，點選同意按鈕 (Agree)。

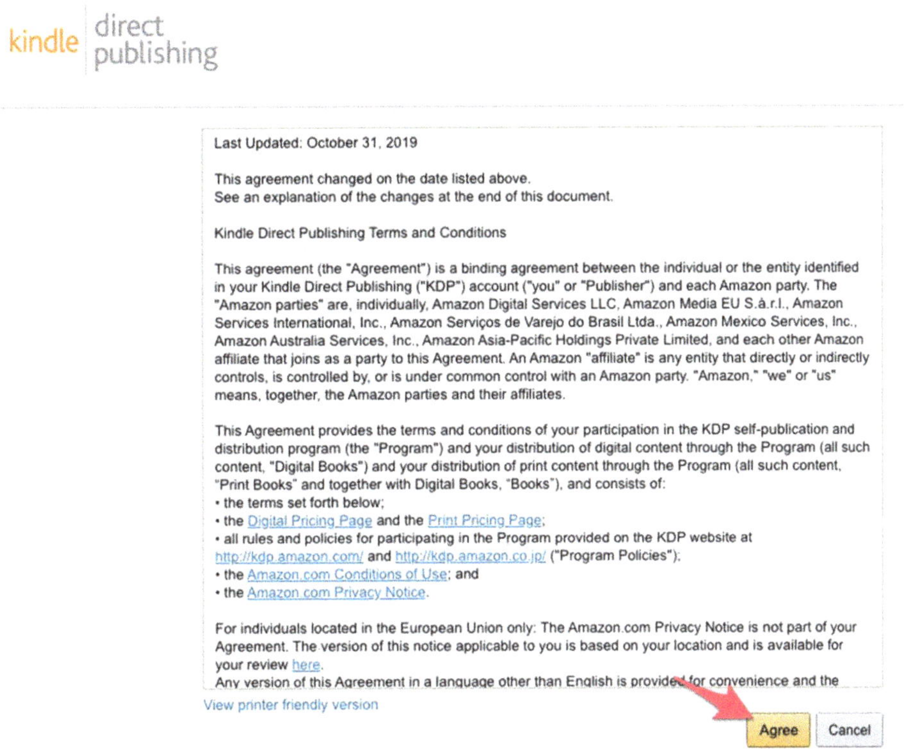

kindle | direct publishing

Last Updated: October 31, 2019

This agreement changed on the date listed above.
See an explanation of the changes at the end of this document.

Kindle Direct Publishing Terms and Conditions

This agreement (the "Agreement") is a binding agreement between the individual or the entity identified in your Kindle Direct Publishing ("KDP") account ("you" or "Publisher") and each Amazon party. The "Amazon parties" are, individually, Amazon Digital Services LLC, Amazon Media EU S.à.r.l., Amazon Services International, Inc., Amazon Serviços de Varejo do Brasil Ltda., Amazon Mexico Services, Inc., Amazon Australia Services, Inc., Amazon Asia-Pacific Holdings Private Limited, and each other Amazon affiliate that joins as a party to this Agreement. An Amazon "affiliate" is any entity that directly or indirectly controls, is controlled by, or is under common control with an Amazon party. "Amazon," "we" or "us" means, together, the Amazon parties and their affiliates.

This Agreement provides the terms and conditions of your participation in the KDP self-publication and distribution program (the "Program") and your distribution of digital content through the Program (all such content, "Digital Books") and your distribution of print content through the Program (all such content, "Print Books" and together with Digital Books, "Books"), and consists of:
• the terms set forth below;
• the Digital Pricing Page and the Print Pricing Page;
• all rules and policies for participating in the Program provided on the KDP website at http://kdp.amazon.com/ and http://kdp.amazon.co.jp/ ("Program Policies");
• the Amazon.com Conditions of Use; and
• the Amazon.com Privacy Notice.

For individuals located in the European Union only: The Amazon.com Privacy Notice is not part of your Agreement. The version of this notice applicable to you is based on your location and is available for your review here.
Any version of this Agreement in a language other than English is provided for convenience and the

View printer friendly version

Agree   Cancel

之後亞馬遜會帶你到 KDP(Kindle Direct Publishing)的後台，也就是發佈書籍的後台，到這一步我們還沒有完全設定好帳號，還要點選下圖上方的 Update Now，去完整的填上自己的資料。

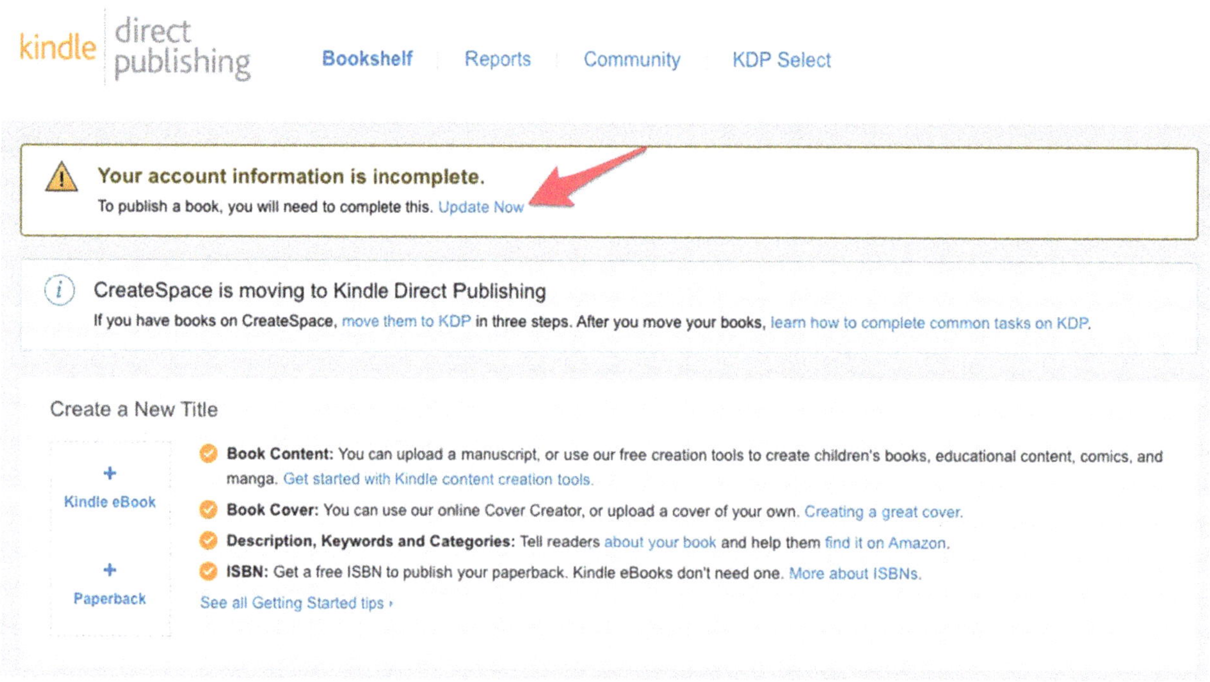

按下 Update Now 後，會來到如下圖的畫面，有三個部份需要填寫：

Author/Publisher Information，如果你是個人的話，也就是填上你自己的基本資料，如果是公司的話，可填上公司名稱與其資料。如果不知道自己地址的英文，可以[按這裡到中華郵政查詢](#)。

Your Royalty Payments，即亞馬遜付給你佣金的方式，如果您沒有美國的銀行帳戶，請按右邊的"I don't have a bank"，

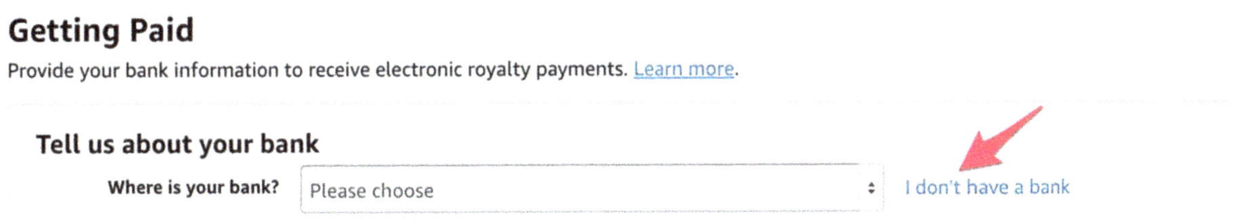

Getting Paid

Provide your bank information to receive electronic royalty payments. Learn more.

Tell us about your bank

Where is your bank?   Please choose   ⇕   I don't have a bank

系統會自動把佣金支付方式改為支票，並顯示可收到貨幣種類，如下圖。

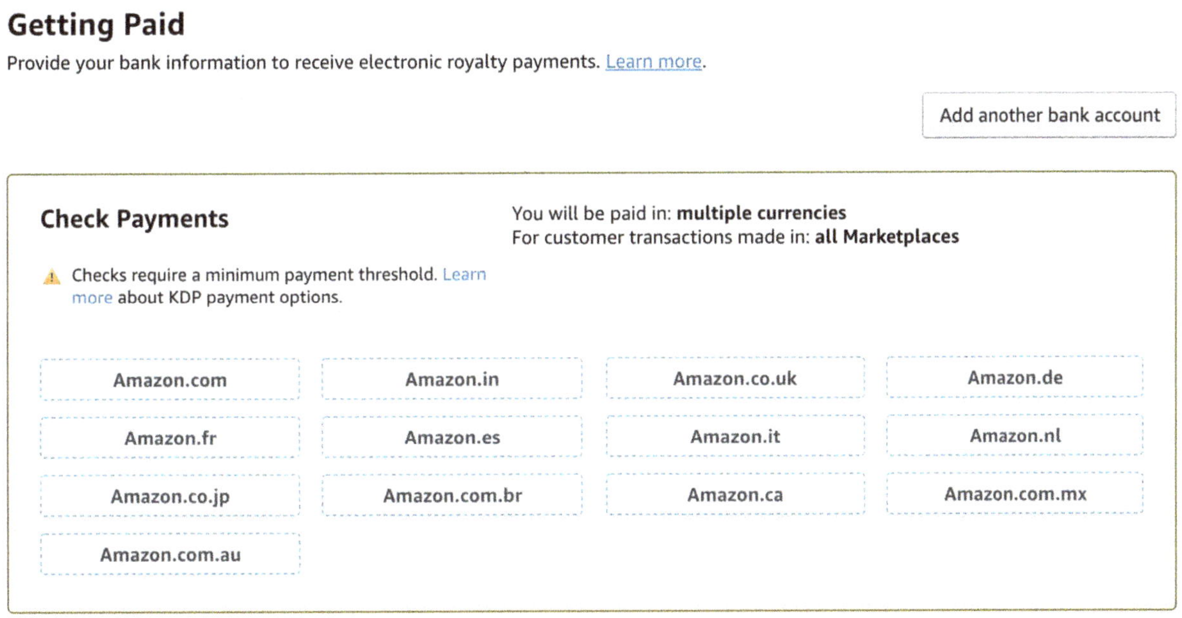

Getting Paid

Provide your bank information to receive electronic royalty payments. Learn more.

Add another bank account

Check Payments

⚠ Checks require a minimum payment threshold. Learn more about KDP payment options.

You will be paid in: **multiple currencies**
For customer transactions made in: **all Marketplaces**

Amazon.com	Amazon.in	Amazon.co.uk	Amazon.de
Amazon.fr	Amazon.es	Amazon.it	Amazon.nl
Amazon.co.jp	Amazon.com.br	Amazon.ca	Amazon.com.mx
Amazon.com.au			

Tax Information 個人稅務資訊，按左下的橘黃按鈕進入稅務資訊填寫頁面，如下圖：

Tax Information

Complete payment setup: Tax withholding

Before we can send you payments, we need to collect some tax info about your business. You will be redirected to our secure tax platform, and then returned here for confirmation.

Complete Tax Information

Save

Tax Information Interview

About You

What is your tax classification?

選擇個人或公司，一般來說選個人即可

Individual   Business

"Individual" includes Sole Proprietors or Single-Member LLCs where the owner is an individual

For U.S. tax purposes, are you a U.S. person?

是否為美國人

Yes   No

Are you acting as an intermediary agent, or other person receiving payment on behalf of another person or as a flow-through entity?

是否由第三方代填，自行填寫請選 No

Yes   No

Tax Identity Information   稅籍資料

Full name ⓘ
Evelyn Cox   填上你的護照上英文全名

Country Of Citizenship ⓘ
Taiwan   選擇台灣   ⌄

Address

Permanent Address ⓘ   填上您的永久地址
#13, Aly 5, Ln 426 Wo-long St.
Taipei, Taiwan 110
Taiwan

[Edit]

Mailing address ⓘ
☑ Same as Permanent Address

勾選郵寄地址是否為永久地址
不是的話,請不要勾選,輸入
您的郵寄地址

Tax Identification Number (TIN)

☑ I have a Non-US TIN   勾選 I have a Non–US TIN   ☐ I have a U.S. TIN

TIN Value ⓘ
A123456789   輸入身分證字號

Provide the Tax ID issued to you by your country of tax residency

ⓘ **Why am I asked for U.S. TIN?**
By providing a valid U.S. TIN, you may be eligible for
reduced withholding tax rate.

[Continue]   點選繼續

之後需要選擇你稅籍地,如台灣,完成後再點擊 Confirm 按鈕繼續。

Claim of Tax Treaty Benefits

You may be eligible to receive a reduction in the 30% US tax withholding rate by providing the information below.

選擇你的稅籍地區   ⓘ

Country of Tax Residence

Taiwan   ⌄

The selected country does not qualify for treaty benefits.

[Confirm]

Sign and Submit

勾選我同意使用電子簽章

☑ I consent to provide electronic signature for the information provided as per IRS Form W-8BEN

ⓘ If you provide an electronic signature, you will be able to submit your tax information immediately.

Under penalties of perjury, I declare that I have examined the information on this form and to the best of my knowledge and belief it is true, correct, and complete. I further certify under penalties of perjury that:

1. I am the individual that is the beneficial owner (or am authorized to sign for the individual that is the beneficial owner) of all the income to which this form relates or am using this form to document myself for chapter 4 purposes,

2. The person named on line 1 of this form is not a U.S. person,

3. The income to which this form relates is: (a) not effectively connected with the conduct of a trade or business in the United States, (b) effectively connected but is not subject to tax under an applicable income tax treaty, or (c) the partner's share of a partnership's effectively connected income,

4. The person named on line 1 of this form is a resident of the treaty country listed on line 9 of the form (if any) within the meaning of the income tax treaty between the United States and that country,

5. For broker transactions or barter exchanges, the beneficial owner is an exempt foreign person as defined in the instructions, and

6. I agree that I will submit a new form within 30 days if any certification made on this form becomes incorrect.

Furthermore, I authorize this form to be provided to any withholding agent that has control, receipt, or custody of the income of which I am the beneficial owner or any withholding agent that can disburse or make payments of the income of which I am the beneficial owner.

The Internal Revenue Service does not require your consent to any provisions of this document other than the certifications required to establish your status as a non-U.S. individual and, if applicable, obtain a reduced rate of withholding.

Signature (Type your full name)

輸入你護照上的英文名字

Evelyn Cox

By typing my name on the given date, I acknowledge I am signing the tax documentation under penalties of perjury.

Date

11-07-2019

You can modify the date to a day before or after to fit your timezone.

點擊Save and Preview繼續

[Save and Preview]

之後後出現填寫資料讓你預覽，如下圖：

Form **W-8BEN**	**Certificate of Foreign Status of Beneficial Owner for United States Tax Withholding and Reporting (Individuals)**	**SUBSTITUTE** (July 2017)

Do NOT use this form if:

	Instead, use Form:
• You are NOT an individual	W-8BEN-E
• You are a U.S. citizen or other U.S. person, including a resident alien individual	W-9
• You are a beneficial owner claiming that income is effectively connected with the conduct of trade or business within the U.S. (other than personal services)	W-8ECI
• You are a beneficial owner who is receiving compensation for personal services performed in the United States	8233 or W-4
• A person acting as an intermediary	W-8IMY

Part I **Identification of Beneficial Owner**

1 Name of individual who is the beneficial owner

Evelyn Cox

2 Country of citizenship

Taiwan

3 Permanent residence address (street, apt. or suite no., or rural route). **Do not use a P.O. box or in-care-of address.**

#13, Aly 5, Ln 426 Wo-long St.

City or town, state or province. Include postal code where appropriate.

Taipei Taiwan 110

Country

Taiwan

4 Mailing address (if different from above)

City or town, state or province. Include postal code where appropriate.

Country

5 U.S. taxpayer identification number (SSN or ITIN), if required (see instructions)

6 Foreign tax identifying number (see instructions)

A123456789

Part II **Claim of Tax Treaty Benefits**

9 I certify that the beneficial owner is a resident of within the meaning of the income tax treaty between the United States and that country.

10 **Special rates and conditions** (if applicable—see instructions): The beneficial owner is claiming the provisions of __ of the treaty identified on line 9 above to claim a _%_ rate of withholding on (specify type of income): _

Explain the additional conditions in the Article and paragraph the beneficial owner meets to be eligible for the rate of withholding:

Part III **Certification**

Under penalties of perjury, I declare that I have examined the information on this form and to the best of my knowledge and belief it is true, correct, and complete. I further certify under penalties of perjury that:

1. I am the individual that is the beneficial owner (or am authorized to sign for the individual that is the beneficial owner) of all the income to which this form relates or am using this form to document myself for chapter 4 purposes.
2. The person named on line 1 of this form is not a U.S. person,
3. The income to which this form relates is (a) not effectively connected with the conduct of a trade or business in the United States, (b) effectively connected but is not subject to tax under an income tax treaty, or (c) the partner's share of a partnership's effectively connected income,
4. The person named on line 1 of this form is a resident of the treaty country listed on line 9 of the form (if any) within the meaning of the income tax treaty between the United States and that country, and
5. For broker transactions or barter exchanges, the beneficial owner is an exempt foreign person as defined in the instructions.

Furthermore, I authorize this form to be provided to any withholding agent that has control, receipt, or custody of the income of which I am the beneficial owner or any withholding agent that can disburse or make payments of the income of which I am the beneficial owner. **I agree that I will submit a new form within 30 days if any certification made on this form becomes incorrect.**

The Internal Revenue Service does not require your consent to any provisions of this document other than the certifications required to establish your status as a non-U.S. individual and, if applicable, obtain a reduced rate of withholding.

Sign Here

Evelyn Cox	11-07-2019	
Signature of beneficial owner (or individual authorized to sign for beneficial owner)	Date (MM-DD-YYYY)	Capacity in which acting

Above is preview of your tax form based on the information you have provided. Please review and submit the form, or make changes if needed.

Make Changes	Submit Form

點擊 Submit Form 後繼續，會出現如下圖，則代表帳號已完全申請完畢。

Tax Information Interview

代表稅務資料送出成功

✓ **Validated**
Your tax information has been received and successfully validated.

Applicable Withholding Rate : 30.0%

點擊離開

Exit Interview

退出稅務資訊後系統回到以下畫面，點選"Bookshelf"，

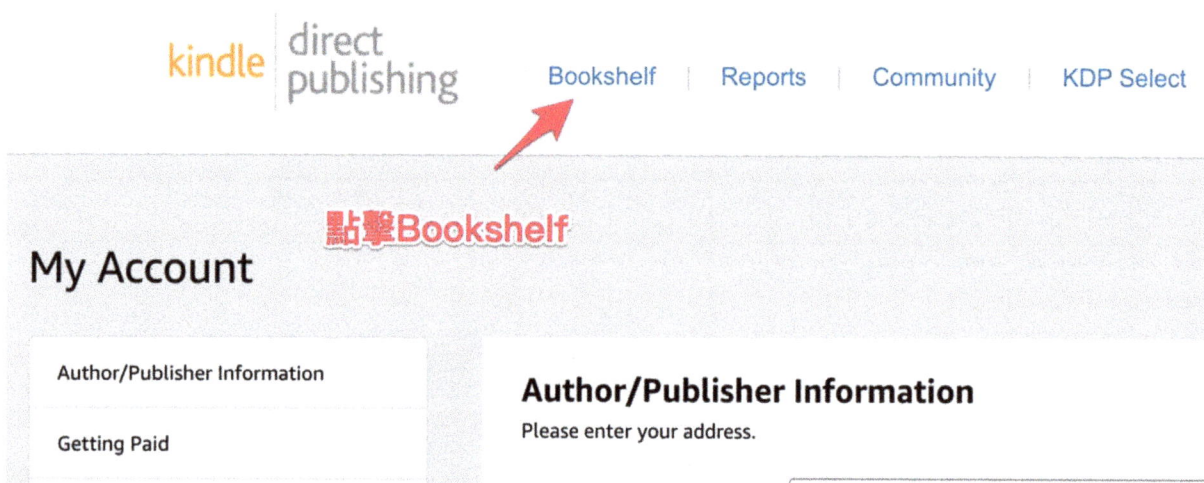

kindle direct publishing   Bookshelf | Reports | Community | KDP Select

點擊Bookshelf

My Account

Author/Publisher Information

Getting Paid

Author/Publisher Information
Please enter your address.

若沒有任何警告，如下圖：

就代表你已經成功註冊亞馬遜 KDP 電子書發佈平台，下一步就是開始上架你的電子書了！

電子書上架

打開瀏覽器後，在網址列上輸入 http://kdp.amazon.com ，如果你已經註冊好帳號的話，你會看到亞馬遜 KDP 的後台如下，我們點選螢幕上方選項的 Bookshelf(書架)後，再點選 Kindle eBook (新增電子書)的連結。

之後我們會看到下列畫面，有三大部分，第一個是電子書的詳細資料英文叫做：Kindle eBook Details，第二個是書本的內容 Kindle eBook Content，第三個是書本的定價部分 (Kindle eBook Pricing)，我們先從 Kindle eBook Details 開始來：

Language(語言)

首先我們要選擇您電子書內容的主要語言-在這邊我以中文來做示範。

Kindle eBook Details
✓ Complete

Kindle eBook Content
✓ Complete

Kindle eBook Pricing
i Not Started...

Language

Choose your eBook's primary language (the language in which the book was written). Learn more about languages supported on Kindle. ▾

Chinese (Traditional) (Beta)

目前中文電子書只支援Microsoft Word檔案
且只有橫向閱讀之方式

i KDP currently supports only Microsoft Word (doc or docx) files for eBooks written in Chinese (Traditional).
Chinese (Traditional) on KDP is currently in beta. Only horizontal content is supported.

Book Title(書名)

首先我們要做的就是把書名打上去，如上圖紅色箭頭處，在 Book Title 打上你自己電子書的書名，書名副標 Subtitle 可填可不填。

Book Title

Enter your title as it will appear on the book cover.

Book Title

北海道的奇幻之旅　　輸入書名

Subtitle (Optional)

一段回憶的旅程　　輸入副標 (選填)

系列書(Series)

因為我要上架的書不是一系列的書，所以我在 Series 的選項未填寫，如果你的書是一系列的話，可以輸入系列書名及書號。

Series　The series name and volume number will help customers find other books in your series on Amazon.

Series Information (Optional)　系列書資訊 (選填)

Series name	Series number
系列書名	系列書編號

版本號碼(Edition Number)

可寫可不寫，一般我都不填寫。

Edition Number　You can provide an edition number if this title is a new edition of an existing book. What counts as a new edition? ▾

Edition Number (Optional)　版本號碼資訊 (選填)

輸入版本號碼

作者(Author)

填上這本電子書作者的姓名或筆名，First name: 姓，Last name: 名。

Author

Primary Author or Contributor

Johnny 填寫作者的名	Wang 填寫作者的姓

書的貢獻者(Contributors)

可添加書的貢獻者，如果有其他作者也可以輸入多個或是有 Editor(編輯)，想要把他們都放上去也可以，一般我都不填寫。

Contributors (Optional) 其他書籍貢獻者(選填)

| Author ⬍ | First name | Last name | Remove |

Add Another 新增其他貢獻者

書的敘述(Description)

再來就是書的敘述(Book Description)，如果你隨便找本亞馬遜 Kindle 的電子書來看，它的書的敘述，就是下圖紅色圈起來的部分。

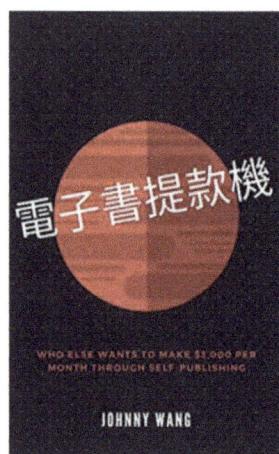

電子書提款機 (Traditional Chinese Edition) Kindle Edition

by 政松 王 (Author)

› See all formats and editions

Kindle
$0.00 kindle unlimited

Read with Kindle Unlimited to also enjoy access to over 1 million more titles
$210.00 to buy

這是一本有關如何在亞馬遜自助出版電子書的一本電子書，如果有興趣，可以買來看看。

Length: 118 pages ⌄   Enhanced Typesetting: Enabled ⌄   Page Flip: Enabled ⌄
Language: Traditional Chinese
Available on these devices ⌄
Due to its large file size, this book may take longer to download

我們就是要把書的敘述當成是書的銷售頁，如果書的敘述寫好了，就把它貼到下圖的 Description 裡:

Description   This will appear on your book's Amazon detail page. Why do book descriptions matter? ▾

我們一家到北海的所發生的趣事與回憶，把這本書留做紀念，希望未來小孩可以看到書的內容！

3958
characters left

電子書版權(Publishing Rights)

電子書版權的問題，因為我們的電子書是自己創作或外包給寫手創作，所以不是屬於 public domain work(公用版權)，所以我們要選第一個選項

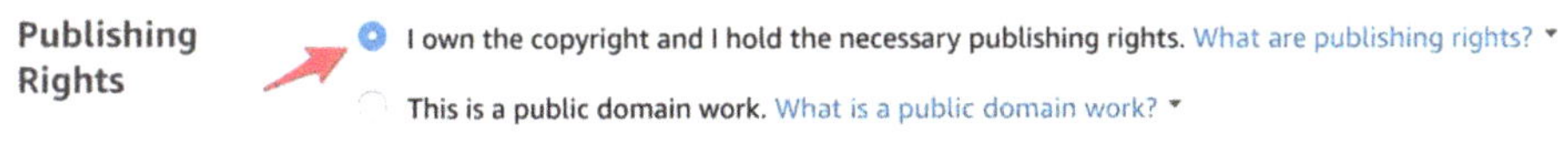

Publishing
Rights

○ I own the copyright and I hold the necessary publishing rights. What are publishing rights? ▼
○ This is a public domain work. What is a public domain work? ▼

關鍵字(Keywords)

再來要填的就是關鍵字，這裡提到的關鍵字是亞馬遜給消費者去搜尋可能會找到的關鍵字，所以一定要填，從下圖我們可以看到亞馬遜提供我們放置最多 7 個跟這本書有關的關鍵字

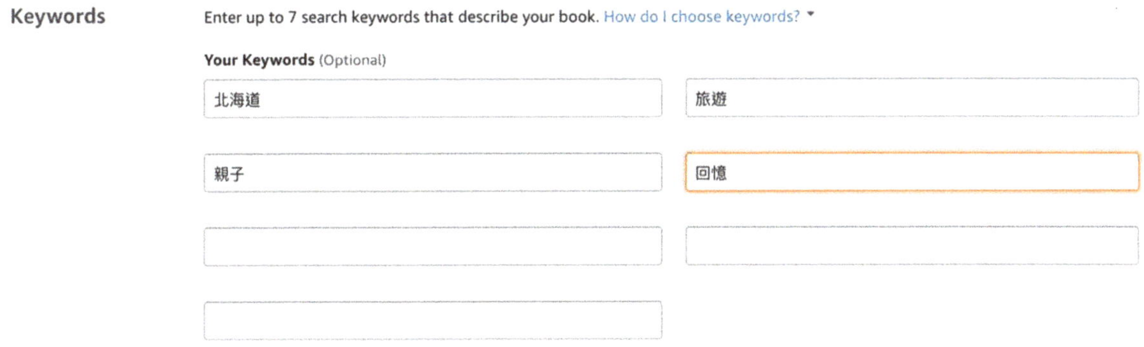

Keywords

Enter up to 7 search keywords that describe your book. How do I choose keywords? ▼

Your Keywords (Optional)

| 北海道 | 旅遊 |
| 親子 | 回憶 |

這一步雖然不是必填，但我強烈建議各位一定要找到 7 個與主題有關的關鍵字把它們填上去，這樣會讓消費者更有機會找到我們的書。

選擇分類(Categories)

再來是要選擇電子書的市場分類，看看我們的電子書是要放到亞馬遜的哪個分類 (Categories)裡去賣，我們可以先去找一些類似的書，看看他們是放在哪些類別裡，如下圖：

Amazon Best Sellers Rank: #118,224 Paid in Kindle Store (See Top 100 Paid in Kindle Store)
#7 in Chinese (Traditional) eBooks
#25 in Biographies of Educators (Kindle Store)
#28 in Family Activities

然後參考他們去選擇我們想要的分類，比如我找的類似的書它是放在 Puzzles & Games 下的 Puzzles，我也可以把我的書放在這個類別裡，首先要做的就是點選下圖的 Categories(選擇電子書分類)

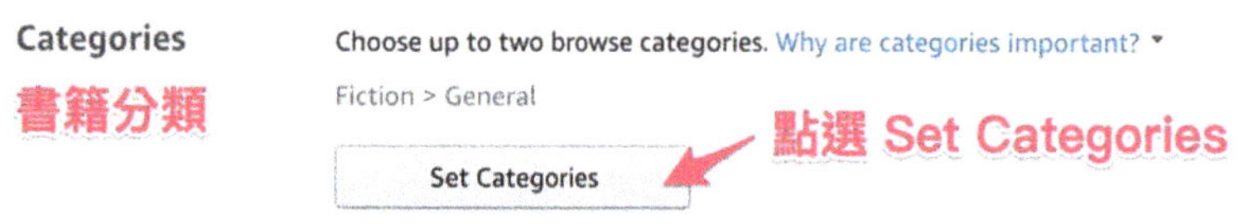

Categories
書籍分類

Choose up to two browse categories. Why are categories important? ▾
Fiction > General

點選 Set Categories

Set Categories

點選 Set Categories 後，會出現許多分類的選項，再去勾選我們想要的類別，如下圖：

Choose up to two categories: ×

Choose categories (up to two):

- ⊞ Cooking
- ⊞ Crafts & Hobbies
- ⊞ Design
- ⊞ Drama
- ⊟ Family & Relationships
  - ☑ General
  - ⊞ Abuse
  - ☑ Activities
  - ☐ Adoption & Fostering
  - ☐ Alternative Family
  - ☐ Anger

Selected categories:

Nonfiction > Family & Relationships > General Remove
Nonfiction > Family & Relationships > Activities Remove

Cancel　Save

在所有的分類裡去找最接近的類別，如: Family & Relationships 裡的 General 與 Activities，之後再點選 Save 儲存起來。

年齡&年級(Age and Grade Range)

如果你的電子書為童書，可選擇適合閱讀的年齡層及年級；一般書籍可省略不填。

Age and Grade Range

Children's book age range (Optional) 兒童書年齡範圍
Age Range

Minimum   Maximum
[Select   ⬍]   [Select   ⬍]

US grade range (Optional) 美國年級範圍
U.S. Grade Range

Minimum   Maximum
[Select   ⬍]   [Select   ⬍]

出版時間(Pre-Order)

一般來說我都設定成第一個選項，馬上出版

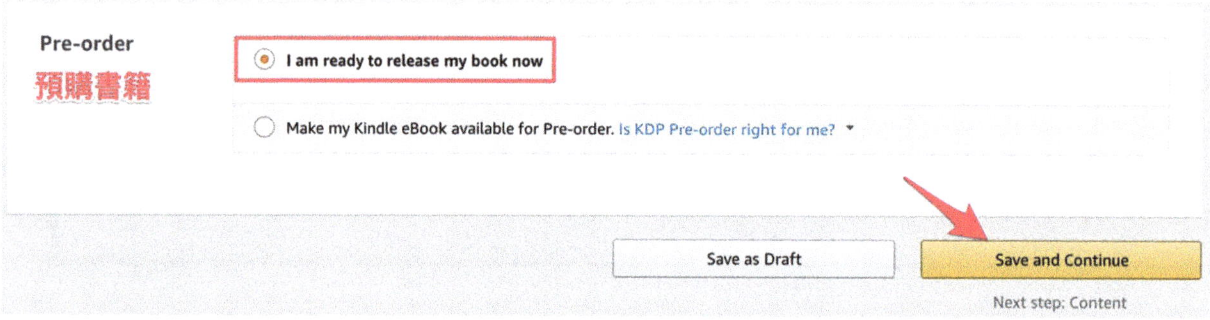

Pre-order
預購書籍

⦿ I am ready to release my book now

◯ Make my Kindle eBook available for Pre-order. Is KDP Pre-order right for me? ▾

[Save as Draft]   [Save and Continue]

Next step: Content

填寫完畢後按上圖箭頭處的 Save and Continue (儲存及繼續) 到下一個部分 Kindle eBook Content。

數位版權管理(DRM)

數位版權管理，一般來說我都是選擇第二個選項，也就是不開啟數位版權管理，這樣聽說比較會讓多一點人看到我們的電子書：

Manuscript   Please read our KDP Content Guidelines and upload a manuscript containing interior content for your Kindle eBook. View supported file types ▼

Digital Rights Management (DRM)
Enable DRM on this Kindle eBook. How is my Kindle eBook affected by DRM? ▼

○ Yes
● No

再來就是上傳電子書內容，點選下圖的 Upload eBook manuscript...

Manuscript   Please read our KDP Content Guidelines and upload a manuscript containing interior content for your Kindle eBook. View supported file types ▼

Digital Rights Management (DRM)
Enable DRM on this Kindle eBook. How is my Kindle eBook affected by DRM? ▼

○ Yes
● No

ⓘ Please upload Microsoft Word (doc or docx) files with horizontal content only

[Upload eBook manuscript]

之後選擇我們要上傳的電子書，記得是我們之前做好的 Microsoft Word 檔案喔，選擇好後再按「開啟」便開始上傳。

亞馬遜需要一些時間做上傳的動作，如下圖，看檔案大小時間不一定

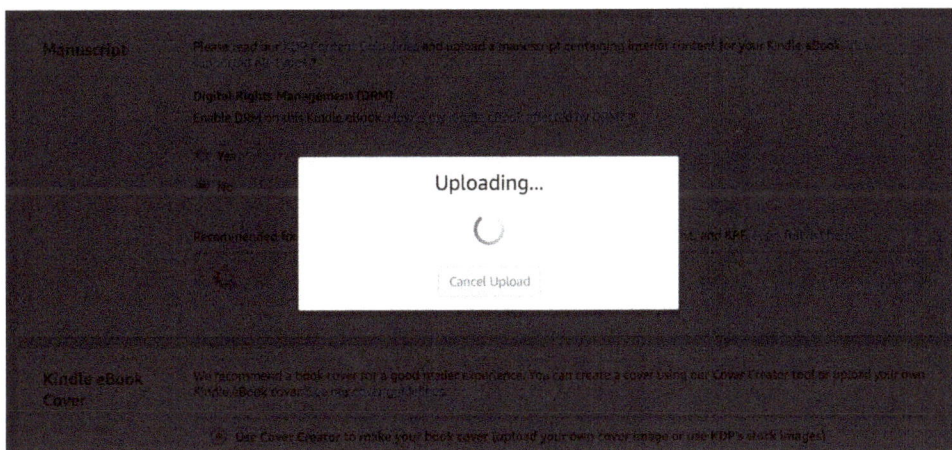

上傳成功後，就會出現 Save Successful! 表示上傳好了。

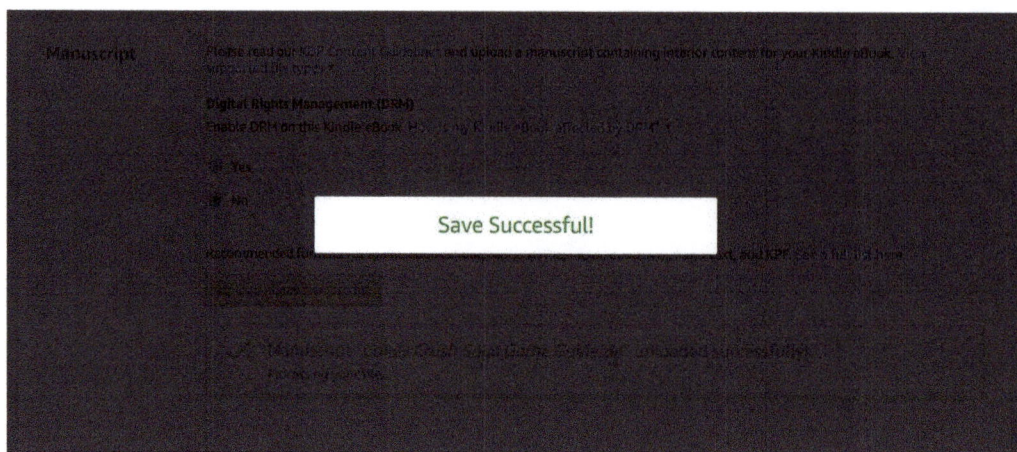

檔案成功上傳後，Amazon 會再花一點時間做拼字檢查，完成後如下圖：

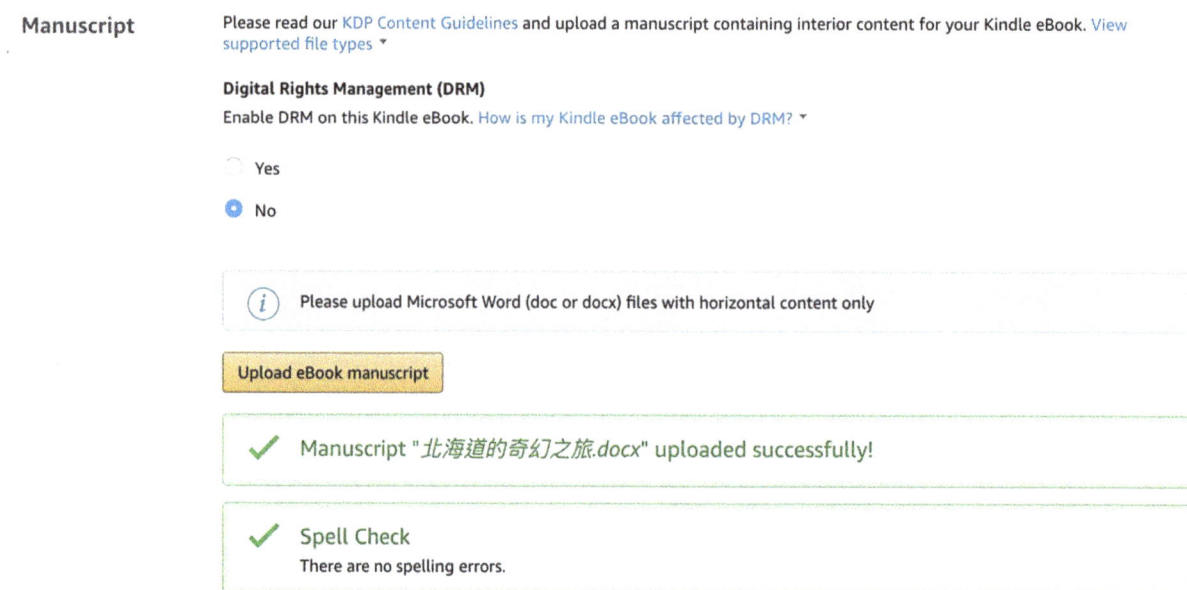

Manuscript	Please read our KDP Content Guidelines and upload a manuscript containing interior content for your Kindle eBook. View supported file types ▾

Digital Rights Management (DRM)
Enable DRM on this Kindle eBook. How is my Kindle eBook affected by DRM? ▾

○ Yes

● No

ⓘ Please upload Microsoft Word (doc or docx) files with horizontal content only

[Upload eBook manuscript]

✓ Manuscript "*北海道的奇幻之旅.docx*" uploaded successfully!

✓ Spell Check
There are no spelling errors.

封面(Kindle eBook Cover)

接下來是電子書封面的上傳，點選下圖的 Upload your cover file 後去找到我們先前設計好的封面檔案(記得要是 .jpg or .tiff 的格式)。

Kindle eBook Cover

We recommend a book cover for a good reader experience. You can create a cover using our Cover Creator tool or upload your own Kindle eBook cover. See our cover guidelines.

○ Use Cover Creator to make your book cover (upload your own cover image or use KDP's stock images)

● Upload a cover you already have (JPG/TIFF only)　　**上傳封面(限JPG/TIFF格式)**

Upload your cover file

✓ Cover uploaded successfully!

成功上傳後，就可以看到封面了，亞馬遜也會顯示 Cover uploaded successfully!

預覽(Kindle eBook Preview)

接著可以去點選 Launch Previewer，如下圖去預覽我們的電子書

Kindle eBook Preview

Online Previewer
The Online Previewer is the easiest way to preview. It lets you preview most books as they would appear on Kindle e-readers, tablets and phones.

Launch Previewer　　**點選 Launch Previewer 預覽書籍**

Downloadable Preview Options

ⓘ Your book cannot be downloaded.

kindle | direct publishing   北海道的奇幻之旅   ▮ ▯

直向或橫向預覽

前後頁按鈕   ‹   ›

泡奶時間到

終於出發了 ...

但是帶著兩個小孩那麼多的行李要坐飛機，其實還是蠻累的，只記得我們也是要早早出發。

到北海道大概有 4 個多鐘頭的飛行時間，我記得到那邊已經是下午時間了。而且我們還要租車再到飯店，不過，不管是租車還是開車都是一種很特別的體驗，反正我也忘記到底開了多久，因為做了一天的飛機已經很累了。到了飯店好不容易終於把行李全部都下了下來，其實已經很累了，但是，那個時候也已經很晚了，兩隻小孩已經準備要喝奶了。

可以點選 ">" 或 "<" 向前或後多看幾頁，也可直向或橫向預覽看看書的內容格式是否 OK，沒問題後就點選上圖左上角箭頭處的 Book Details 繼續

Kindle eBook ISBN

不需要做任何變動，維持內定的設定即可，因為電子書不需要申請 ISBN (國際書碼)。

Kindle eBook ISBN	**ISBN** (Optional) Kindle eBooks are not required to have an ISBN. What is an ISBN? ▾ [ ] **Publisher** (Optional) [ ]

[< Back to Details]   [Save as Draft]   [Save and Continue]

再來按上圖箭頭處的 Save and Continue (儲存及繼續)進入最後一個部分 Kindle eBook

Pricing。

KDP Select Enrollment

勾選 Enroll my book in KDP Select，主要目的是讓更多的亞馬遜客戶可以購買/讀取/借閱我們的電子書，所以一般都會選擇註冊 KDP Select 來最佳化我們的版稅，雖然下圖是勾選的，但是我建議在這個階段先不要勾選，之後我們再說明為什麼。

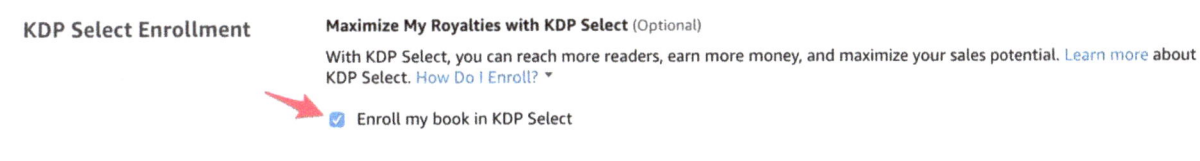

KDP Select Enrollment

Maximize My Royalties with KDP Select (Optional)

With KDP Select, you can reach more readers, earn more money, and maximize your sales potential. Learn more about KDP Select. How Do I Enroll? ▼

☑ Enroll my book in KDP Select

銷售區域(Territories)

這個部分我們要選擇第一個選項，不用懷疑，也就是賣到全世界去賺全世界人的錢。

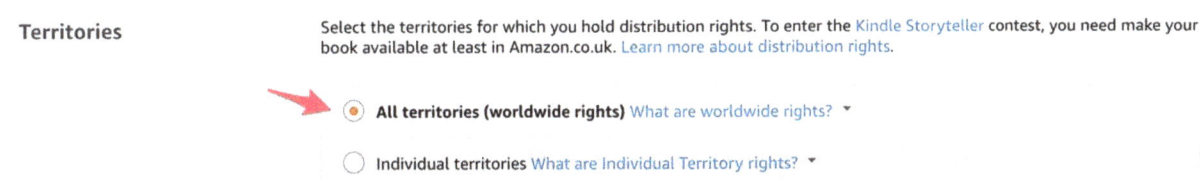

Territories

Select the territories for which you hold distribution rights. To enter the Kindle Storyteller contest, you need make your book available at least in Amazon.co.uk. Learn more about distribution rights.

⦿ **All territories (worldwide rights)** What are worldwide rights? ▼

◯ Individual territories What are Individual Territory rights? ▼

定價(Royalty and Pricing)

再來就是選擇我們要賣的電子書單價，我們先來看一下亞馬遜對定價與版稅的制訂方法為何？

亞馬遜對於電子書版稅佣金的部分有以下兩種:

- 第一種為 35%，電子書賣價介於美金$0.99～$200，每賣出一本書，我們可以賺到35%的版稅佣金，比如說，我們的書賣價為: $0.99 美金，每賣出一本，我們可以賺到的版稅佣金就是:$0.99 x 35% = 約 $0.35 美金，但因為我的這本書裡面含有大量圖片，所以亞馬遜規定我的最低價格要設定在$1.99 美金，所以我每賣出一本可獲取的版稅為：$1.99 x 35% = $0.7 如下圖所示:

Select a royalty plan and set your Kindle eBook list prices below

🔘 35%

⚪ 70%

ℹ️ Your book file size after conversion is 3.44 MB.

Primary Marketplace	List Price			Rate	Delivery	Royalty
Amazon.com ⇕	$ 1.99	USD		35% ▾	$0.00	$0.70
	Must be $1.99-$200.00 ▾			70%	n/a	n/a
	All marketplaces are based on this price					

Other Marketplaces (12)　　　　　　　　　　　　　　　　⌄

- 第二種為 70%，電子書賣價介於美金$2.99～$9.99，每賣出一本書，我們可以賺到 70%的版稅佣金，比如說，我們的書賣價為: $2.99 美金，每賣出一本，我們可以賺 的版稅佣金就是:

$2.99 x 70% = 約 $2 美金，但因為我的這本書裡面含有大量圖片，所以拿到的版稅只有 $1.73，有一部份被吃掉了，那是因為大量圖片的電子書在讀者下載時必須要支付更多的 傳輸費，亞馬遜把這筆費用直接在版稅上夠掉了，如下圖所示:

Select a royalty plan and set your Kindle eBook list prices below

⚪ 35%

🔘 70%

ℹ️ Your book file size after conversion is 3.44 MB.

Primary Marketplace	List Price			Rate	Delivery	Royalty
Amazon.com ⇕	$ 2.99	USD		35% ▾	$0.00	$1.05
	Must be $2.99-$9.99 ▾			70%	$0.52	$1.73
	All marketplaces are based on this price					

Other Marketplaces (12)　　　　　　　　　　　　　　　　⌄

確定好定價後，亞馬遜會自動把在美國的賣價幫我們在其他國家設定好，當然你也可以在每個國家設定不同的賣價。

Select a royalty plan and set your Kindle eBook list prices below

○ 35%

● 70%

ⓘ Your book file size after conversion is 3.44 MB.

Primary Marketplace	List Price		Rate	Delivery	Royalty
Amazon.com ⇅	$ 2.99	USD	35% ▾	$0.00	$1.05
	Must be $2.99-$9.99 ▾ All marketplaces are based on this price		70%	$0.52	$1.73

Other Marketplaces (12) ⌃

Amazon.in	₹ 212	INR	70%	₹24	₹109
	Must be ₹69-₹10999 ▾ Based on Amazon.com	₹180 without IN VAT			
Amazon.co.uk	£ 2.33	GBP	70%	£0.34	£1.12
	Must be £1.99-£9.99 ▾ Based on Amazon.com	£1.94 without UK VAT			
Amazon.de	€ 2.99	EUR	70%	€0.41	€1.47
	Must be €2.99-€9.99 ▾ Based on Amazon.com	€2.51 without DE VAT			
Amazon.fr	€ 2.99	EUR	70%	€0.41	€1.69
	Must be €2.99-€9.99 ▾ Based on Amazon.com	€2.83 without FR VAT			

電子書借閱(Book Lending)

這裡的電子書借閱與 KENP 不同，如果我們有勾選的話，表示購買我們的書的消費者可以把他買的電子書借給他朋友閱讀最多到 14 天，這個我一定都勾選，因為如果有其他人有喜歡我們的書的話，可以增加我們的銷售量。

註：當版稅選擇 70%時，亞馬遜會強制勾選電子書借閱功能。

其他都沒有問題後，同意亞馬遜電子書出版發佈的條款與條件，在點選 Publish Your Kindle eBook 就完成電子書上架了。

接下來我們會看到下面畫面，表示亞馬遜正在發佈我們的電子書

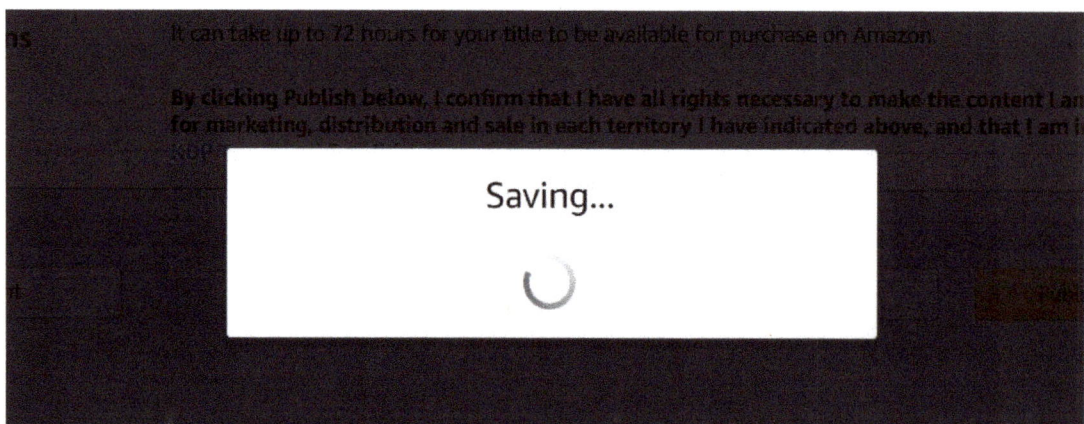

完成後如果看到下面畫面就代表我們已經成功的發佈我們的電子書了，

亞馬遜會顯示需要 72 小時去做審核，點擊 Done 後會直接回到以下畫面。

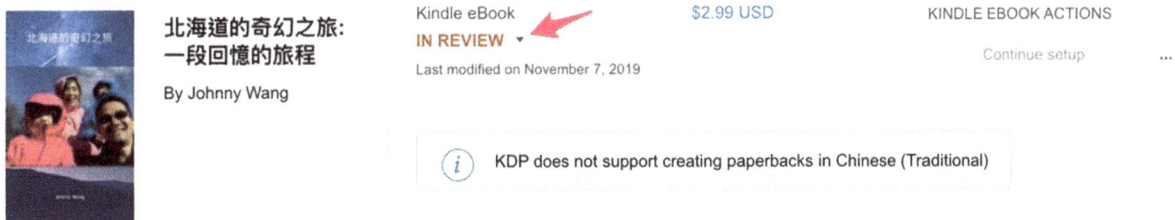

到這一步我們已經完成電子書的上架了。電子書上架完成後，亞馬遜需要一些時間去審核，在電子書的狀態列 (Status) 會顯示 In Review，如果已經審核通過狀態列會變成 Publishing，表示正在出版上架到亞馬遜商城中，最後一步，如果看到 Live 表示我們已經完成電子書的出版了，就等著收版稅吧

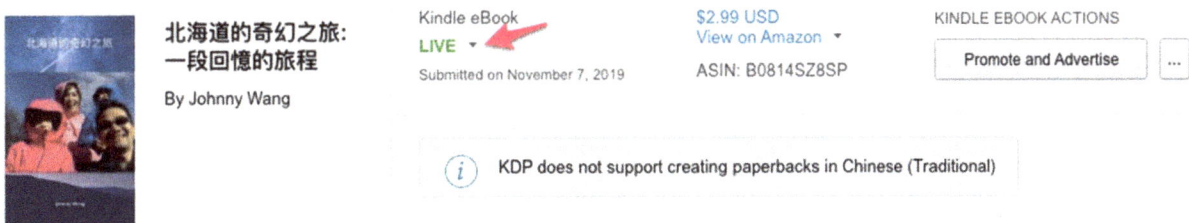

電子書行銷 - 怎麼賣?

KDP Select

到底甚麼是 KDP Select，我們先前有提到，亞馬遜有個會員服務叫做 Amazon Prime，凡是參加了這個服務的亞馬遜會員都可以享有每個月免費租借電子書的服務，亞馬遜把這項會員免費租借電子書的服務特別叫做 Kindle Owners' Lending Library (KOLL)，之後亞馬遜又推出了 Kindle Unlimited，也就是如果你有參加 Amazon Prime 的話，可以每個月無限制的租借電子書，完全不用錢。

如果我們的電子書有加入 KDP Select 這項服務計畫的話，我們的書就有機會被這些有參加 Amazon Prime 的會員租借，只要是被租借了，看租的人把我們的書看了幾頁，亞馬遜就會每頁的版稅佣金發給我們。

亞馬遜每個月提撥的金額不一定，實際提撥金額會顯示在 KDP 的後台如下圖，2019 年 11 月亞馬遜提撥了 2,590 萬美金要發放給這些參加 KDP Select 的電子出版商

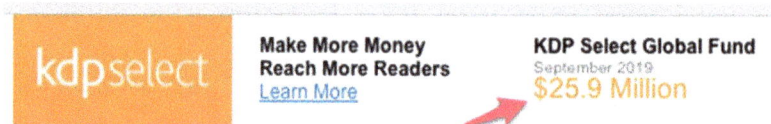

之前我會建議我們所有的電子書都要參加 KDP Select 的服務，有時候我們賺到的 KOLL 租借版稅佣金會比實際賣出的佣金還多，但是因為亞馬遜在 2015 年 7 月修改了規則，由原本只要被租借一本書就可以賺到租借的版稅佣金，變成了要讀者租借你的書後要讀取頁數後的每一頁數版稅佣金，根據我的經驗，租借的佣金少了約 3-4 成，有些月份少更多，現在我會建議除了試試看 KDP Select 也可以試試把書上架到 Smashwords 或是 Digital2Draft。

參加 KDP Select 的唯一缺點是，亞馬遜限制從我們的電子書參加 KDP Select 起的 90 天，我們的電子書禁止到其他的平台販售，而且亞馬遜每 90 天會自動幫我們延續參加 KDP Select 的計畫，所以如果我們有計畫把電子書放到其他平台做販售，就必須自己取消參加 KDP Select 計畫。

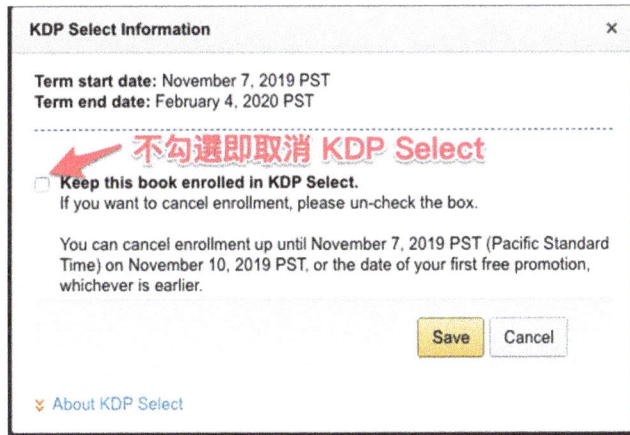

註冊 KDP Select

如果我們的電子書的狀態列已經到了 Publishing 或是 Live 的階段，我們應該可以看到在最右側有一灰色...按鈕，將滑鼠移到如下圖箭頭後，會出現許多選項，這裏有一欄位叫做 Enroll in KDP Select，可以點選加入 KDP Select 計畫，如下圖:

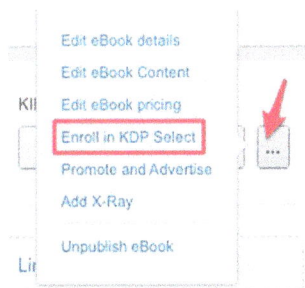

點選之後會出現下面的畫面:

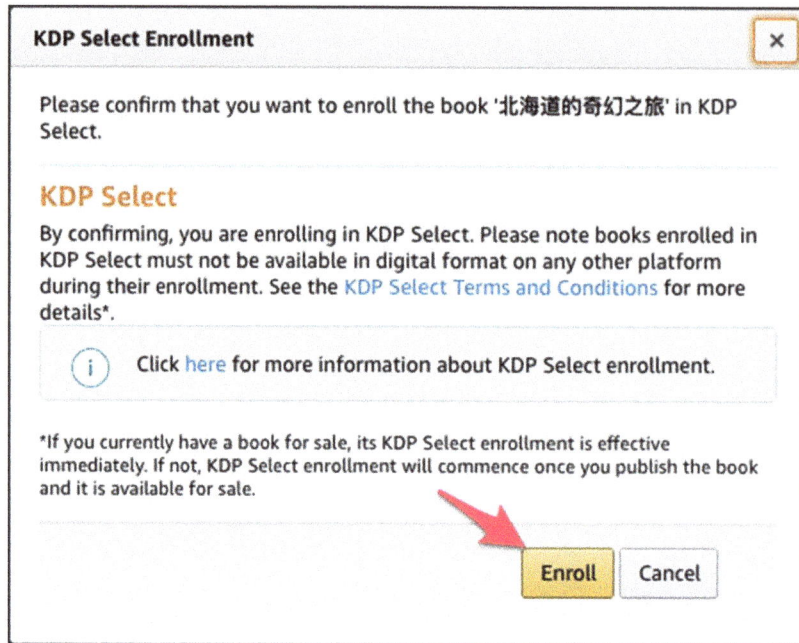

點擊 Enroll，則會出現以下畫面，Your Current KDP Select Status: Enrolled，代表你的書已經
註冊參加 KDP Select 成功！

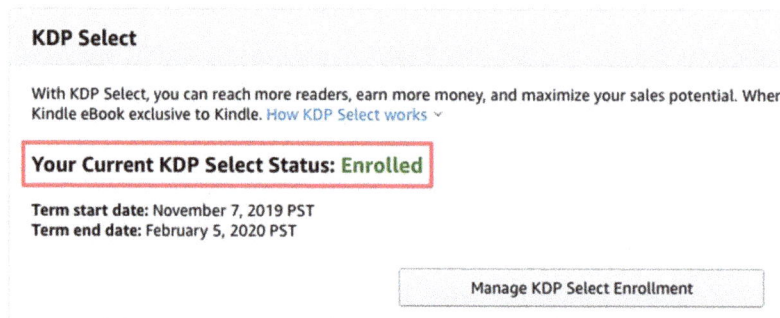

如果你在上架電子書的時候有注意到應該會看到有這樣的一個畫面

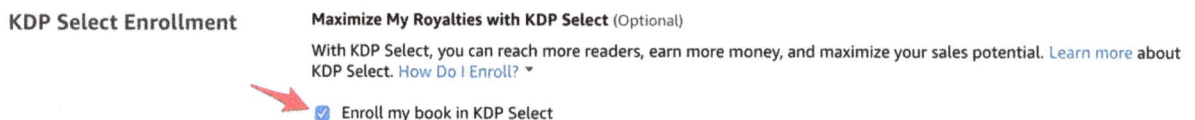

這是在上架電子書也可以先勾選參加 KDP Select 的計畫，但是我建議在我們的電子書已經到了 Publishing 或是 Live 的階段，再來勾選參加這服務，原因是因為如果你先勾選了 KDP Select 的選項，有可能你的電子書在被亞馬遜審核時會認為你的書有版權問題，即使你是請寫手做全新的創作，亞馬遜還是有可能不讓你參加這項計畫，這樣我們就會損失賺取租借電子書 (KU/KOLL/KENP) 的版稅佣金，如果你的電子書沒有通過 KDP Select 的計畫，你去點選 Enroll 的話，會出現下面的畫面，意思就是說你的電子書有版權問題無法參加 KDP Select 計畫。

KDP Select Enrollment

You have chosen the book '▒▒▒▒▒ ▒▒▒▒ ▒▒▒▒ ▒ ▒▒▒▒ ▒▒▒▒▒▒ ▒▒ ▒▒▒▒ ▒▒▒▒▒ ▒▒▒ ▒▒ ▒▒▒▒▒▒▒▒' which does not qualify for enrollment in KDP Select because either you do not have exclusive rights for the primary content of this book (i.e., this content is in the public domain or others may also have the right to publish this content) or your book is not exclusive to Amazon. See the KDP Select FAQ for more information. To re-enroll a book that was previously removed from KDP Select and is now exclusive, please contact us.

Close

這也是我建議在我們的電子書已經到了 Publishing 或是 Live 的階段，再來勾選參加 KDP Select 這項服務。

設定免費下載排程

參加 KDP Select 有另外一個好處，就是亞馬遜會為我們的電子書做免費的行銷，亞馬遜提供我們的電子書在 90 天內有 5 天讓消費者可以免費下載，可能你會覺得很奇怪為什麼我們的電子書要提供給別人免費下載，其實這 5 天的免費下載對我們的電子書是非常的有幫助，尤其是我們的書剛出版時更有幫助。

因為我們的書剛出版上架到亞馬遜平台的時候，並不是很多人知道我們的書，亞馬遜上有上百萬本電子書要讓消費者找到我們的書也不容易，所以這時候可以利用這 5 天免費下載來為我們的電子書做行銷，越多人下載我們的電子書，我們電子書的排名就會越高，如下圖有一本電子書在免費下載時的最高排名是: #66,776，

Amazon Best Sellers Rank: #66,776 Free in Kindle Store (See Top 100 Free in Kindle Store)
#19 in 30-Minute Travel Short Reads
#5 in Japanese Travel
#16 in Travel in German

當這本書在免費下載的時間裡被下載的次數越多，排名就越高，等到免費下載的時間結束後，這本書還是可以享有高排名的蜜月期，這個時候就會被許多的消費者看到這本書，有興趣的人就會去購買，所以就可以賺更多的版稅佣金。

要如何設定這 5 天的免費下載時間呢? 我建議當我們的電子書只要一通過亞馬遜的審核，電子書的狀態列變成是 Live 的時候，我們馬上就去參加 KDP Select 計畫，之後就勾選我們想要設定免費下載的電子書然後點選 Promote and Advertise，如下圖:

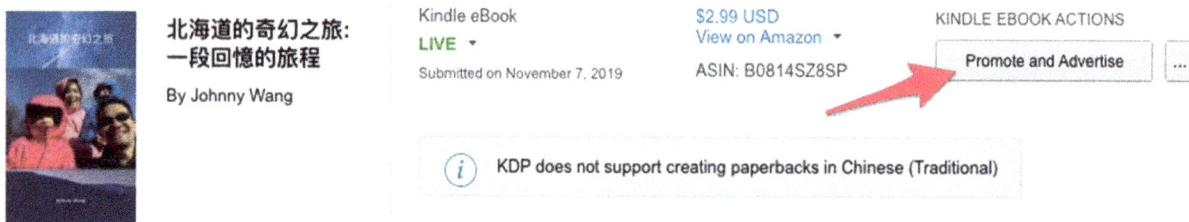

北海道的奇幻之旅:
一段回憶的旅程
By Johnny Wang

Kindle eBook
LIVE ▾
Submitted on November 7, 2019

$2.99 USD
View on Amazon ▾
ASIN: B0814SZ8SP

KINDLE EBOOK ACTIONS
Promote and Advertise   ...

ⓘ KDP does not support creating paperbacks in Chinese (Traditional)

點選選項後，會出現如下圖的畫面

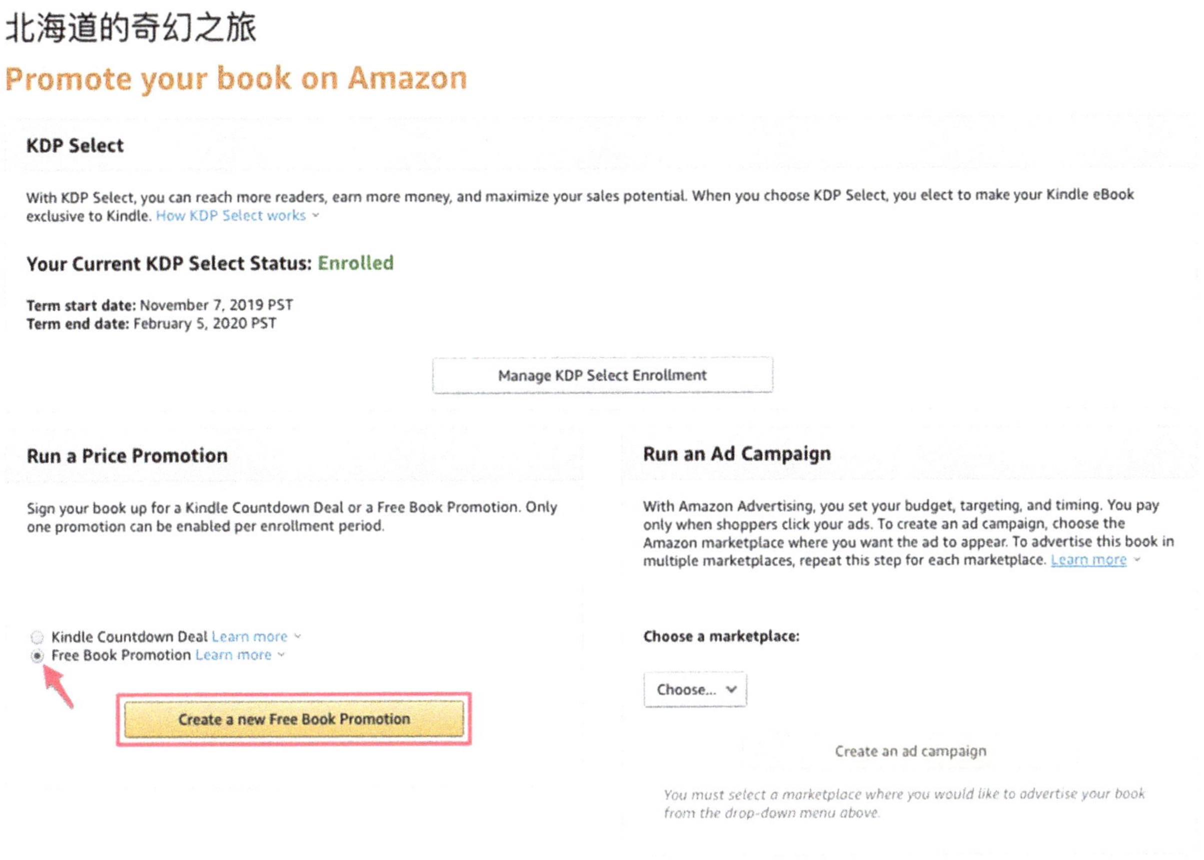

北海道的奇幻之旅

我們要的是圈選左手邊 Run a Price Promotion 裡的 Free Book Promotion 這個選項，之後點擊 Create a new Free Book Promotion 按鈕後會出像我們可以排程的畫面如下圖，

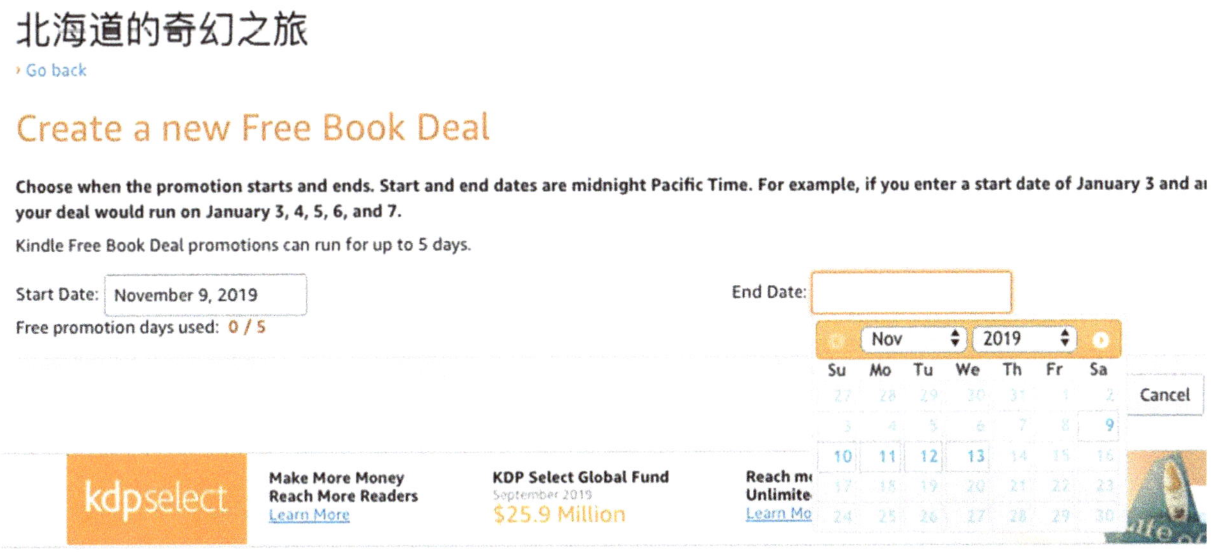

再來就把要設定的排程時間輸入，比如說，設定的時間為 Nov/09/201 到 Nov/13/2019 為期 5 天，然後按 Save Changes 儲存

北海道的奇幻之旅
› Go back

Create a new Free Book Deal

Choose when the promotion starts and ends. Start and end dates are midnight Pacific Time. For example, if you enter a start date of January 3 and an end date of January 7, your deal would run on January 3, 4, 5, 6, and 7.

Kindle Free Book Deal promotions can run for up to 5 days.

Start Date: November 9, 2019   End Date: November 13, 2019
Free promotion days used: 5 / 5

Cancel   Save Changes

設定完成後可以看到如上面的畫面，在左下角處有 Free promotion days used: 5/5，意思就是有 5 天的排程，我已經用了 5 天。

如果要修改時間的話就點選右邊的 Edit 去修改時間或 Delete 把這排程取消。

Promotions & Advertisements for this book

All ∨

Benefit Type	Marketplace	Start	End	Status	
Free Book Promotion		Saturday, November 9, 2019, 12:00 AM PST	Wednesday, November 13, 2019, 11:59 PM PST	Scheduled	› Edit › Delete

電子書定價

再來我們要談的是電子書的定價，我們前面有提到亞馬遜對於電子書版稅佣金的部分有以下兩種：電子書賣價介於美金$0.99~ $200，每賣出一本書，我們可以賺到 35%的版稅佣金，電子書賣價介於美金$2.99 ~ $9.99，每賣出一本書，我們可以賺到 70%的版稅佣金，在電子書上的定價會與我們選定的利基市場有關，比如說一般來說童書的訂價都不是很高，所以許多出版商對他們頁數不是很多的童書會定在$0.99 美金，這個訂價策略有兩個目的：

- 提高電子書的排名
- 賺 KU/KOLL 的版稅佣金

有些時候$0.99 對某些消費者而言是很少的錢，所以低售價的電子書通常賣的數量會比較多，這是心理學上的衝動購買(Impulse buying)，就是消費者認為這本書很便宜，不管看不看或用不用的到，先買了再說，這對我們出版商來說當然是一個不錯的策略，只是定價在$0.99 我們每賣出一本只賺$0.35 確實是少了點。

所以這也是為什麼我們要參加 KDP Select 的原因之一，因為在美國有許多人的擁有 Kindle 電子書閱讀器。

這些擁有 Kindle 的消費者只要是有參加 Amazon Prime 的服務都可以免費下載參加 KDP Select 的電子書，出版商設定定價為$0.99 有時候是為了得到更多的租借版稅，因為$0.99 的書會被許多人衝動購買，所以排名就會提高，排名提高了之後，就會被更多消費者看到，這時候許多這些 Kindle 擁有者看到這些書就會利用這項服務去下載，對我們個人出版商而言我們就可以賺取 KU/KOLL/KENP 版稅佣金。

一般來說，電子書剛出版的時候，我自己會設定書的定價為$2.99 或$3.99，如果在蜜月期賣得好的話，我就可以賺到更多的佣金，如果我的排名下降了，我就會把價錢改成$0.99 去衝排名，如果排名又衝上來的話，再把定價改成$2.99 或$3.99，就是重複這樣的步驟來達到賺取最多版稅佣金的可能，如下圖：

電子書排名

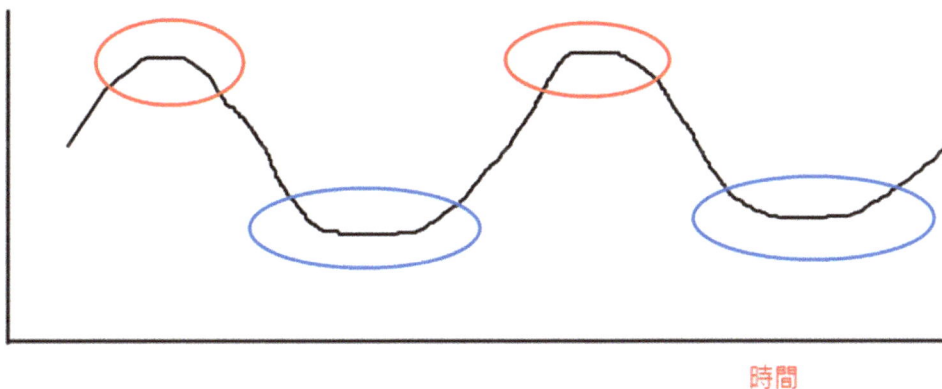

時間

電子書再排名高的時候如上圖紅色圈圈時，設定較高的電子書單價($2.99 或$3.99)，排名下降時如藍色圈圈時，設定較低的電子書單價($0.99)。

上面所說的是一個大方向的策略，有的時候必須要花時間去測試每本書最好的定價已達到最佳化的收入，要更改電子書的定價步驟如下：

點選 KDP 後台的 Bookshelf 後

選我們想要變更價錢的書，然後到右邊點選 Edit eBook pricing：

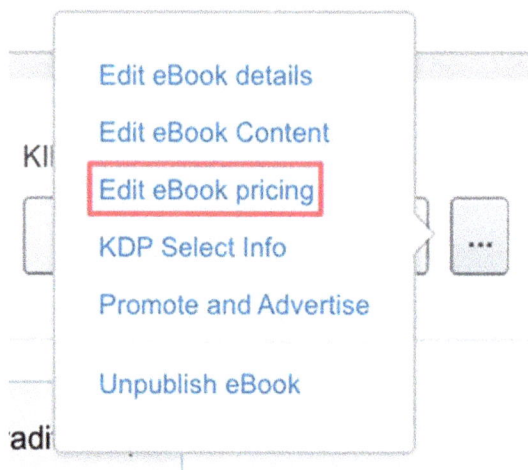

KDP 後台會帶我們來的設定價錢的部分，先選擇我們要的版稅％後，再去設定書的價錢

Royalty and Pricing

KDP Pricing Support (Beta)
See the relationship between price and past sales and author earnings for KDP books like yours.

View Service

i KDP Pricing Support is not available because we don't have enough data

Select a royalty plan and set your Kindle eBook list prices below

○ 35%
● 70%

i Your book file size after conversion is 3.44 MB.

Primary Marketplace	List Price		Rate	Delivery	Royalty
Amazon.com ⇕	$ 2.99	USD	35% ▾	$0.00	$1.05
	Must be $2.99-$9.99 ▾		70%	$0.52	$1.73
	All marketplaces are based on this price				

Other Marketplaces (12) ⌄

設定好之後，再把捲軸拉到最下面，在箭頭處打勾然後點選 Publish Your Kindle eBook 就完成了

< Back to Content		Save as Draft	Publish Your Kindle eBook

之後亞馬遜會顯示需要 72 小時去做審核，要回到 KDP 後台再點選 Close 按鈕就可以了。

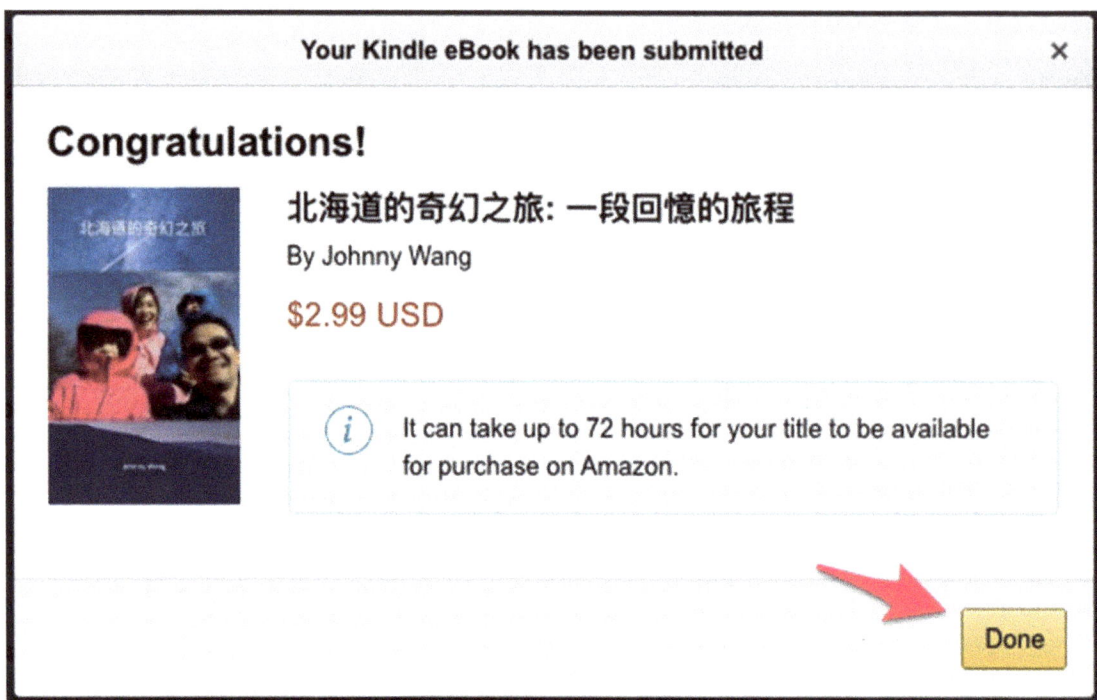

Your Kindle eBook has been submitted   ✕

Congratulations!

北海道的奇幻之旅: 一段回憶的旅程

By Johnny Wang

$2.99 USD

ⓘ It can take up to 72 hours for your title to be available for purchase on Amazon.

Done

成功者的秘密

大家好，很開心可以和大家分享亞馬遜 KDP 電子書的經驗。在這邊你已經學會了如何利用亞馬遜平台來創造更多的被動收入，但最重要的成功者的心態，在這我也跟大家分享一下利用電子書賺錢所應具備的心態：

一定時間的工作與一定的努力

舉例來說，我個人喜歡打高爾夫球，所以會花一定的時間練球與一定的努力尋求突破。想要從電子書賺被動收入也是一樣，學習製作電子書賺錢的過程可能是很辛苦的，但要告訴自己這是成功者所需具備的心態，不要想找到很快就能賺到錢的方式 (雖然說利用亞馬遜已經是很快可以從網路上賺到錢的方法)，想一步登天，天下沒有白吃的午餐。所有成功者都是經過一定時間的工作與一定的努力，才達到一定的收入。

不要預期自己馬上可以賺到錢

網路賺錢不能快速致富，但卻是人人都可以做到的。以我自身的經驗發現，網路真的可以讓你很簡單賺到錢。但簡單不代表容易，如果你想要賺很多錢，它也許不是來得那麼得快，也許有人花一年、兩年，有人花三年，四年但他們最終都可以從網路上賺到很多人的錢。各位照著我的經驗做，我相信你一定也可以賺到你想要賺的錢。

把電子書賺錢或網路賺錢當成一門事業

把自己當作是個生意人，不可能都不付出就想要有收入，這裡跟大家分享的是，如何用最小的投資，獲得最大的利潤。網路賺錢迷人之處在於它的投資是非常非常少的。舉例來說，一本書成本$10 美金，但它可以讓我賺到$500 美金，甚至更多。如果有 10 本這樣的書，月收入就是$5,000 美金！

與加盟便利商店或是飲料店、咖啡店、餐廳等相比，他們的加盟金可能是好幾百萬，而且你不知何時才能回收，但如果你投資 10 本書，如果說一本書的成本是 NT$1,500，也不過1.5 萬台幣左右，跟幾百萬相比已經差很多了，如果把方法用得好甚至可以把成本壓的更低，而會來的每個月是可以有$200 美金，$500 美金甚至更高的收入。利用電子書賺錢是不斷的把佣金給賺進來，它是一個真正的被動收入。

目標設定

做任何事都要設定目標。如果沒有設定目標，就像你矇著眼睛射箭，不知道要往哪射。目標設定的好處在於可以照著我們的目標，做好時間管理，完成我們想要做的事。目標設定可以採取以下原則：

SMART 原則

目標設定要把握 SMART 原則：

- S: Specific ， 目標是具體明確的

- M: Measure ， 目標是可以衡量的

- A: Achievable ， 目標是可以達到的

- R: Realistic ， 目標是實際的

- T: Timely ， 目標要有時間表

以電子書舉例來說：

[我要在 12 個月內製作 50 本電子書，每本電子書平均賺 20 美金相當於月入 1,000 美金或 30,000 台幣。] (紅色字代表是在目標設定中，一定要有的設定)。

這樣的話就知道每個月要出版約 50/12 = 約 4.16 本電子書，這樣看起來好像還蠻 ok 的，但是實際上可不可行呢？

根據我的經驗，因為並不是我們所有出版的電子書都賣得動，也許我們的成功率是 60%，也就是說出版 10 本書，有 6 本賣得動，這樣計算的話每個月便需要出版到 4.16/60% = 6.9，有就是大約 7 本電子書，所以在本我們的目標重新設定一下：

[我要在 12 個月內製作 84 本電子書，每月平均上架 7 本電子書，每本電子書平均賺 20 美金相當於月入 1,000 美金或 30,000 台幣。]很好…=>擊敗 22k!!!恭喜。

看起來這好像很不容易，但這是新手非常好的一個目標設定，有可能你的書會大賣，也許平均每本每月可以賺到$50-$60 美金，這樣只要 20-30 本就可以達到了。你可以自己親身體驗後看看有沒有哪些需要調整的，然後在把目標重新設定一下。原則上，我會鼓勵大家先上 10 本書去感受一下整個電子書賺錢的流程。運氣好的話，可能 3-4 個月後，就有可能月入上千美金了。最重要的是，希望大家可以互相合作，互相分享經驗，跟一群有心的人一起學習。

最後這大家順利，勇敢地採取行動去開創你的電子書事業吧，加油！

線上出版高階課程

我們的線上出版高階課程，有超過 100 個影片，帶你一步步操作整個流程，並教你更多如何出版**實體書**如圖畫書，著色繪本...等等，如果你對我們的線上出版高階課程有興趣，請點擊下方連結:

我要知道更多有關線上出版課程的資訊

亞馬遜電子書行銷快速起步指南

1. 先把電子書提款機 PDF 檔案閱讀至少 2 次

2. 找出 20 個大主題

3. 嚴選出 10 個利基市場

4. 製作第一個利基市場內容大綱(TOC)

5. 註冊與熟悉外包平台(Upwork , Guru)

6. 發佈寫手職缺到各個外包平台

7. 錄用寫手(Ghostwriter)

8. 確認寫手提交內容

9. 確認書名(研究其他已出版之相關書籍名稱)

10. 電子書檔案編輯

11. 電子書封面製作

12. 電子書製作(封面+內容)

13. 註冊亞馬遜 KDP 平台

14. 上傳電子書

15. 等待亞馬遜審核

16. KDP Select 免費下載排程

17. 重複步驟 1-16 直到上架 10 本書